READ ME
AND LAUGH

A Funny Poem for Every Day
of the Year

Also chosen by Gaby Morgan

Read Me 1
A Poem for Every Day of the Year

Read Me 2
A Poem for Every Day of the Year

Frogs in Clogs
A World Book Day Poetry Book

READ ME AND LAUGH

A Funny Poem for Every Day of the Year

Chosen by Gaby Morgan

MACMILLAN
CHILDREN'S BOOKS

For Gillian Beau-Wright and everyone at King's – Irene,
Milla, Anya, Tammy, Laura, Steve, Jessica Joy,
D'Artagnan, Indiana, Ellie and Amy

First published 2005 by Macmillan Children's Books
a division of Macmillan Publishers Limited
20 New Wharf Road, London N1 9RR
Basingstoke and Oxford
www.panmacmillan.com

Associated companies throughout the world

ISBN 0 330 43557 4

1 3 5 7 9 8 6 4 2

A CIP catalogue record for this book is available from the British Library.

Typeset by SX Composing DTP, Rayleigh, Essex
Printed and bound in Great Britain by
Mackays of Chatham plc, Chatham, Kent.

Contents

January

February

March

April

May

July

August

September

October

November

December

January

New Year Resolution

It was January the 1st
I turned over a new leaf
It was clean on the top side
But had bugs underneath.

Steve Turner

Fire Guard

My wife bought a fire guard for the living room
Seems a nice sort of chap.

Roger McGough

Ettykett

My mother knew a lot about manners,
   she said you should never slurp;
you should hold your saucer firmly,
   and not clang your teeth on the curp.

My father knew nothing of manners,
    all he could do was slurp;
and when I can't find a rhyming word,
    I set about making them urp.

John Rice

Gift

Flat, under the mat
Like a pressed violet
In a lady's book
There is a vole.
Its body curled like a flower
Its tail a thin, thin stem.
It is my gift to you
And you will hate it
Almost as much as I think it wonderful.
That's because you are stupid
And I am a cat.

Jan Dean

Today, I Feel

Today, I feel as:

Pleased as PUNCH,
Fit as a FIDDLE,
Keen as a KNIFE,
Hot as a GRIDDLE,
Bold as BRASS,
Bouncy as a BALL,
Keen as MUSTARD,
High as a WALL,
Bright as a BUTTON,
Light as a FEATHER,
Fresh as a DAISY,
Fragrant as HEATHER,
Chirpy as a CRICKET,
Sound as a BELL,
Sharp as a NEEDLE,
Deep as a WELL,
High as a KITE,
Strong as a BULL,
Bubbly as BATH WATER,
Warm as WOOL,

Clean as a new PIN,
Shiny as MONEY,
Quick as LIGHTNING,
Sweet as HONEY,
Cool as a CUCUMBER,
Fast as a HARE,
Right as RAIN,
Brave as a BEAR,
Lively as a MONKEY,
Busy as a BEE,
Good as GOLD,
Free as the SEA.

I'M SO HAPPY – I'M JUST LOST FOR WORDS.

Gervase Phinn

A Bit of a Low Point

Reflected a top mountaineer:
'I've had a successful career.
Alas, as I plummet
From off this high summit,
I guess it's all downhill from here.'

Graham Denton

Icy Morning Haikus

On a frozen pond
a small dog is nervously
  attempting to skate

  Way up in a tree
a black cat grins with delight
  watching and waiting

  Beneath the clear ice
a big fish wonders if all
  dogs walk on water

James Carter

The Dragon Who Ate Our School

1

The day the dragon came to call,
she ate the gate, the playground wall
and, slate by slate, the roof and all,
the staffroom, gym, and entrance hall,
and every classroom, big or small.

So . . .
She's undeniably great.
She's absolutely cool,
the dragon who ate
the dragon who ate
the dragon who ate our school.

2

Pupils panicked. Teachers ran.
She flew at them with wide wingspan.
She slew a few and then began
to chew through the lollipop man,
two parked cars and a transit van.

Wow . . . !
She's undeniably great.
She's absolutely cool,
the dragon who ate
the dragon who ate
the dragon who ate our school.

3

She bit off the head of the head.
She said she was sad he was dead.
He bled and he bled and he bled.
And as she fed, her chin went red
and then she swallowed the cycle shed.

Oh . . .
She's undeniably great.
She's absolutely cool,
the dragon who ate
the dragon who ate
the dragon who ate our school.

4

It's thanks to her that we've been freed.
We needn't write. We needn't read.
Me and my mates are all agreed,
we're very pleased with her indeed.
So clear the way, let her proceed.

Cos . . .
She's undeniably great.
She's absolutely cool,
the dragon who ate
the dragon who ate
the dragon who ate our school.

5

There was some stuff she couldn't eat.
A monster forced to face defeat,
she spat it out along the street –
the dinner ladies' veg and meat
and that pink muck they serve for sweet.

But . . .
She's undeniably great.
She's absolutely cool,
the dragon who ate
the dragon who ate
the dragon who ate our school.

Nick Toczek

Letters to the Three Pigs
(Found in a Gingerbread Filing Cabinet, at the
'King Of The Castle' Planning Office)

Dear Mr Pig, We notice
You've built a house of straw.
You didn't ask permission,
You didn't say what for,
You didn't ring our office,
You didn't write, and so –
Our Big Bad Wolf will be RIGHT ROUND
To huff and puff and blow.

Dear Pig & Co., We're puzzled.
Some creatures never learn.
You've built a house of wooden planks –
The sort that's bound to burn,
The sort that's full of woodworm,
The sort that causes trouble –
Our Big Bad Wolf will be RIGHT ROUND
To smash your place to rubble.

Pig Partners, Now you've done it.
You're either rude or lazy.
You've gone and built a house of bricks
To drive our planners crazy.
You didn't dig foundations,
You knew we'd have to ban it –
Our Big Bad Wolf will be RIGHT ROUND
To blast you off the planet.

Dear Brothers Pig, Our greetings!
We huffed, we puffed, we blew,
We even stormed your chimney,
But NOTHING bothered you –
Our Big Sad Wolf will be RIGHT ROUND
To pay you our respects,
And offer you a splendid job
With Beanstalk Architects.

Clare Bevan

Chalk and Cheese

as different as chalk and cheese they say
but there's plenty of things
that are a lot more different than these
a blade of grass
and a pair of glass dungarees
for instance.

John Hegley

What Teachers Wear in Bed

It's anybody's guess
what teachers wear in bed at night,
so we held a competition
to see if any of us were right.

We did a spot of research,
although some of them wouldn't say,
but it's probably something funny
as they look pretty strange by day.

Our head teacher's quite old fashioned,
he wears a Victorian nightshirt,
our sports teacher wears her tracksuit
and sometimes her netball skirt.

That new teacher in the infants
wears bedsocks with see-through pyjamas,
our Deputy Head wears a T-shirt
he brought back from the Bahamas.

We asked our secretary what she wore
but she shooed us out of her room,
and our teacher said, her favourite nightie
and a splash of expensive perfume.

And Mademoiselle, who teaches French,
is really very rude,
she whispered, 'Alors! Don't tell a soul,
but I sleep in the . . . back bedroom!'

Brian Moses

12

Purrfect

Aaaa

When
you're
smitten by
a kitten, what's
your option?
One
adoption!

Liz Brownlee

13

Love Letter

I hold my breath,
drop the letter on his desk,
watch him pick it up,
mouth the words he reads
following as his finger traces them.

> 'Dear Rodger
> I love you
> love from Alison.'

He looks up
and I can read nothing in his eyes;
picks up his pencil,
shields paper with his arm.
I pray Miss Forshaw isn't looking.

The folded note begins its journey
– Godfrey – Colin – John – Carol –
I wrench it open, desperate to know.

> 'Dear Alison
> There is no d in Roger.'

Alison Chisholm

I Saw a Jolly Hunter

I saw a jolly hunter
With a jolly gun
Walking in the country
In the jolly sun.

In the jolly meadow
Sat a jolly hare.
Saw the jolly hunter.
Took jolly care.

Hunter jolly eager –
Sight of jolly prey.
Forgot gun pointing
Wrong jolly way.

Jolly hunter jolly head
Over heels gone.
Jolly old safety-catch
Not jolly on.

Bang went the jolly gun.
Hunter jolly dead.
Jolly hare got clean away.
Jolly good, I said.

Charles Causley

Practical Science

Do you remember 'Science',
with weird Mr McPhee,
who said, 'My boomerang's
amazing: throw it, curves
back, catch it, watch
and see.' Threw it, curved
back, caught it. 'Easy-
peasy as can be.'
Threw it, curved back,
turned to answer me . . .
Woke up in *Casualty*.

Mike Johnson

Fairy-tale Princess School
Wednesday's Timetable

9.30 a.m. Christening Curses
This week: Methods of waking from enchanted sleep
without having to rely on a princely kiss.
(Several princesses have been disappointed
in the quality of prince thus obtained.)

10.30 a.m. How to recognize your Frog Prince
Princesses are forbidden to kiss the study frogs.
Princess Florabella kissed a frog in last week's lesson
and not only is she in hospital with salmonella poisoning
but got an extremely ugly prince into the bargain.

11 a.m. Break
Crowns are NOT to be worn in the playground.
Grudge the caretaker sustained a nasty flesh wound
when he sat on one which had been left on a bench.

11.15 a.m. Programming your mobile
An essential art if your father, the King,
stakes you out as bait for the local dragon.
A simple press of a button
will contact the knight in shining armour of your choice.

12 Midday Lunch

A light, but nutritious meal of thirty-four courses will be
  provided.
Do not speak to wicked enchanters outside the school gates
as the Princes' Union has called a strike
to protest about the practice of chopping princes' heads off
if they do not achieve tasks set by beautiful, but cruel
  princesses.
(these gels give princesses a bad name)
So there will be no one to rescue you
from the enchanters' towers till further notice.

2 p.m. Disguises

Today we are doing goosegirl, beggarmaid, kitchen skivvy
  and tattercoat,
all tried and tested by well-known princesses and
enabling even a novice to net a handsome prince.

2.30 p.m. Wicked stepmothers

Is your stepmother really an ogress? Has she a magic mirror?
Does she favour your two ugly stepsisters?
This is the first in a series of talks given by famous
  personalities.
Today, it's Snow White.
And remember, your highnesses, do not mention dwarves.
That business was all in the past.

3.30 p.m. Home-time
As paparazzi from various fairyland tabloids
have been pestering princesses as they clamber
into their golden carriages,
we have hired a wizard to blast them with his staff.
This should stop the nuisance
and highnesses are asked not to kick the resultant blackened
  bones
all over Grudge's clean courtyard.

Homework
We must ask princesses not to make their maids do it.
The maids are achieving better marks than their mistresses
and we all know what happens when maids get the upper
  hand.
They will impersonate you and marry your princes
and then where will you be?

Marian Swinger

Cemetery Epitaph

'Please mark my grave
with just one flower.'
That was the wish of
Cynthia Tower.
So when she died
they raised a plinth
and marked upon it

'Hiya, Cynth!'

Wes Magee

My Spectacular Adventure

I have just returned from
that strange
and dangerous world

Called:
The Other Side of Dave's Glasses
Where
pavements rear up at your face
stairs fall away into space
and pointy-headed aliens
catch your bus to school.
Where
lamp posts dance in a mist
while cars swirl and twist
and your bus ticket
begins to unspool.
Where
the flies are the size of mice
and blurry girls look quite nice
and walls wobble
like ripples in a pool.
Where
a scaly, tentacled thing
opens a crocodile mouth to sing
'You've got my specs on
upside down, you fool!'

John Coldwell

19

Batty about Bats

I'm batty about
bats.
I'm head-over-heels in love with
somersaults.
Encores leave me crying out for
more.
I think that flying insects' joints are the bee's
knees,
And that Oxygen is a
gas . . .
But ice-cubes leave me
c-c-cold.

Philip Ardagh

You are Old, Father William

'You are old, Father William,' the young man said,
'And your hair has become very white;
And yet you incessantly stand on your head –
Do you think, at your age, it is right?'

'In my youth,' Father William replied to his son,
'I feared it might injure the brain;
But, now that I'm perfectly sure I have none,
Why, I do it again and again.'
'You are old,' said the youth, 'as I mentioned before,
And have grown most uncommonly fat;
Yet you turned a back-somersault in at the door –
Pray, what is the reason of that?'

'In my youth,' said the sage, as he shook his grey locks,
'I kept all my limbs very supple
By the use of this ointment – one shilling the box –
Allow me to sell you a couple?'

'You are old,' said the youth, 'and your jaws are too weak
For anything tougher than suet;
Yet you finished the goose, with the bones and the beak –
Pray, how did you manage to do it?'

'In my youth,' said his father, 'I took to the law,
And argued each case with my wife;
And the muscular strength, which it gave to my jaw,
Has lasted the rest of my life.'

'You are old,' said the youth, 'one would hardly suppose
That your eye was as steady as ever;
Yet you balanced an eel on the end of your nose –
What made you so awfully clever?'

'I have answered three questions, and that is enough,'
Said his father. 'Don't give yourself airs!
Do you think I can listen all day to such stuff?
Be off, or I'll kick you downstairs!'

Lewis Carroll

Fall in love

Fall in love with Lorna,
  Fall in love with Sam,
Fall in love with Lucy,
  Fall in love with Pam.

Fall in love with Margaret,
　　Fall in love with Frances,
Fall in love with Diane –
　　Wow, the way she dances!

Fall in love with Laura.
　　Fifi's fine as well.
Fall in love with Phoebe, even
　　Though she cannot spell.

Fall in love with Leila,
　　Fall in love with Lou,
Fall for Jo, Fiona, Jane
　　Or any of that crew.

Fall in love with who you like
　　As deeply as you dare.
But brace your heart for breaking:
　　Love is never fair.

Fall in love with any girl
　　While you're on the shelf
But don't fall in love with Jenny, no –

Jenny's in love with herself.

Fred Sedgwick

My Stepdad is an Alien

I'd suspected for some time.
I finally got up the courage
to talk to him about it.

I think you're an alien, I told him.

Nonsense, he said. Why do you think that?

You're bald. You don't have any hair
anywhere.

That's not that unusual, he said.

Well, you've got one green eye
and one blue one.

That doesn't make me an alien, he replied.

You can make the toaster work
without turning it on.

That's just a trick, he smiled.

Sometimes I hear you
talking to Mum in a weird alien language.

I'm learning Greek
and Mum lets me practise on her.

What about your bright blue tail?

Ah, he said thoughtfully.
You're right, of course.
So, the tail gave it away, did it?

Roger Stevens

Mister Moore

Mister Moore, Mister Moore
Creaking down the corridor.

Uh uh eh eh uh
Uh uh eh eh uh

Mister Moore wears wooden suits
Mister Moore's got great big boots
Mister Moore's got hair like a brush
And Mister Moore don't like me much.

Mister Moore, Mister Moore
Creaking down the corridor.

Uh uh eh eh uh
Uh uh eh eh uh

When my teacher's there I haven't got a care
I can do my sums, I can do gerzinters
When Mister Moore comes through the door
Got a wooden head filled with splinters.

Mister Moore, Mister Moore
Creaking down the corridor.

Uh uh eh eh uh
Uh uh eh eh uh

Mister Moore I implore
My earholes ache, my head is sore
Don't come through that classroom door
Don't come through that classroom door.
Mister Mister Mister Moore
He's creaking down the corridor.

Uh uh eh eh uh
Uh uh eh eh uh

Big voice big hands
Big voice he's a very big man
Take my advice, be good be very very nice
Be good be very very nice
To Mister Moore, Mister Moore
Creaking down the corridor

Uh uh eh eh uh
Uh uh eh eh uh

Mister Moore wears wooden suits
Mister Moore's got great big boots
Mister Moore's got his hair like a brush
Mister Moore don't like me much

Mister Moore, Mister Moore
Creaking down the corridor.

Uh uh eh eh uh
Uh uh eh eh uh

David Harmer

Counting the Stars

It's late at night
and John is counting the stars.

He's walking through the woods
and counting the stars.

The night is clear
and the stars are like salt

on a black tablecloth.
John counts silently,

his lips moving, his head tilted.
It's late at night

and John is counting the stars
until he walks into a tree

that he never saw
because he was counting the stars.

Look at John
lying in the woods.

The woodland creatures are gathering around him laughing

in little woodland voices.

Moral:
Even when you're looking up,
Don't forget to look down.

Ian McMillan

My Father

My father is a werewolf,
Right now, he's busy moulting.
He leaves his hairs on stairs and chairs.
It's really quite revolting.
And if my friends make comments
(For some of them are faddy),
I tell them it's the cat or dog.
I never say it's daddy.

Kaye Umansky

Bump!

Things that go 'bump!' in the night
Should not really give one a fright.
It's the hole in each ear
That lets in the fear,
That, and the absence of light!

Spike Milligan

27

Help!

Dear Mrs Berry
As you are our Headteacher
I thought you should know
That I'm writing you this letter
On the floor under my table
Where I have accidentally on purpose
Dropped my pencil
I need to let you know quite urgently
That our supply teacher, Mr Pigge,
Has gone mad. He ranted and raved at us
Using a lot of shouting and spit
Then he stapled Kieron to the wall
And tied Nicola to the door by her plaits
Now he's looking at me.

Whoops! Nearly got caught then!
Fortunately, when he threw his chair at me
I was still under the table
Sadly it hit the five kids next to me
Sent them flying I can tell you!
I can also report that Lucy
Has been glued to the floor for whispering
And Daniel, Gurteak and Sam
Were dumped in the bins by the boiler house
Jade, Sally and Lackveer are crying
And Josh has been shoved head first
Into the gerbil cage.

Hullo Mrs Berry
I'm writing this from the cupboard where
Ten of us have been locked away
For writing notes in class.
I think Mr Pigge is asleep now
I can probably sneak this note
Through a crack in the back
Hoping that you will find it very quickly.
Please rescue us before home time
Unless it's Maths homework tonight, in which case
Please leave us here till Monday.

Your friend Jack
In year Five.

David Harmer

28

Sunday in the Yarm Fard

The mat keowed
The mow cooed
The bog darked
The kigeon pooed

The squicken chalked
The surds bang
The kwuk dacked
The burch rells chang

And then, after all the dacking and the changing
The chalking and the banging
The darking and the pooing
The keowing and the cooing
There was a mewtiful beaumont
Of queace and pie-ate.

Trevor Millum

In Training

The train is at Born-Ville station.
The whistle wails and we're off to Nappily-Ever-After Land.
It's a Poo-poo train, making its way to Crawley.
All change for Childhood-on-the-Daughter.
Now we are nearly at Little Tantrum.
But things are not going our way.
The train speeds on to Big Tantrum.
The brakes screech and scream to an unscheduled stop.
There is an argument on the line.
And we are so close to the town of Kiss-And-Make-Up.
Suddenly diverted to Sulkington-On-See-Me-Later.
We might have to bypass Middle Pudding and
Head straight to Bed-Stone.
At last we have arrived at TV station.
Passengers are advised to watch out for rubbish.
Thank you for travelling on our one-to-five express!

Andrew Fusek Peters

30

The Blue Room

My room is blue, the carpet's blue
The chairs are blue, the door's blue too.
A blue bird flew in yesterday,
I don't know if it's flown away.

Richard Edwards

Chicken Poxed

My sister was spotty,
Real spotty all over,
She was plastered with spots
From her head to her toes.

She had spots on the parts
That her bathing suits cover,
Spots on her eyelids,
Spots on her nose.

I didn't know chickenpox
Could be so interesting,
It seemed such a shame
To waste all those spots.

So when Jody was sleeping
And no one was looking,
I got a blue pen
And connected her dots.

Valerie Bloom

February

Cabbage

The cabbage is a funny veg.
All crisp, and green, and brainy.
I sometimes wear one on my head
When it's cold and rainy.

Roger McGough

Auntie Betty Thinks She's Batgirl

Auntie Betty pulls her cloak on
And the mask – the one with ears.
Almost ready, check the lipstick.
Wait until the neighbours cheer.
Through the window. What a leap!
She lands right in the driver's seat.
Off she goes with style and grace
To make our world a better place.

Andrea Shavick

Invisible Boy

*I*nvisibility potions take
time to prepare.
When he looked in his mirror . . .
'Yes! I'm not there.'

He pulled off his pyjamas,
'Now my fun can begin.'
Ran straight to his school,
in *invisible* skin.

Once in the playground,
tripped up his worst enemy;
knocked a drink from the hand
of 'teacher's pet' Naomi.

A bully he hated
got shoved hard, in the back.
Our invisible hero threw
balls – landed, 'Thwack!'

All this time (with no clothes on),
he'd grown colder and colder,
but this merely made his plans
bolder and bolder.

Marched into assembly,
stood beside the Headmaster
(so thin is that line
between triumph and disaster).

The Head, with composure,
gave one polite cough.
Invisibility potions
can quickly wear off.

Mike Johnson

The Rival Arrives

Tom, take the baby out the fridge
And put the milk back in.
We know you are not used to him
And think he makes a din,
But I'm afraid he's here to stay
And he is rather cute,
So you'll have to stop insisting
He goes in the car-boot.
And please stop telling all your friends
We bought him in a sale,
Or that he's a free sample
We received in the mail.
He was *not* found in a trolley
At the local Mothercare,
And a family did not give him us
Because they'd one to spare.

You should look on the bright side, Tom.
In just a year or two
You will have someone else to blame
For the wicked things you do.

Brian Patten

Mrs Goodwin's Part-time Job

It was just a part-time job
but the money wasn't bad
and it relieved a housewife's boredom
and stopped her going mad.
Of course it was top secret
and the family mustn't know.
She checked her space-time monitor.
It must be time to go.
'Beam me up,' she bellowed,
'the kids have gone to school,
and my husband's gone to work,
so beam me up, you fools
for the Zoorgs mass on the borders
and the Voorgs wait to attack
and I've got to save a planet
before the kids get back.'
A voice said, 'OK, Captain.
It shouldn't take a sec.'
And in a trice, foot tapping,
she was standing on the deck
of a universe class starship,
twenty kilometres wide.
'Full speed ahead, disintegrators
set to fire,' she cried.

The Voorg fleet ran in terror,
the Zoorgs thought twice and fled.
'And now let's save that planet
and the job's all done,' she said.
They beamed her down at home time
as her four kids clattered in.
She landed in the kitchen
in something of a spin
and started to peel carrots
with her space corps issue knife.
'Poor Mum,' her children cackled,
'what a boring life.'

Marian Swinger

Aunt Brute

Aunt Brute was cute
In a bulldog way
But kissing her was weird
She always took her teeth out first
And hung them in her beard.

Bill Condon

Tutor

A tutor who taught on the flute
Tried to teach two young tooters to toot.
   Said the two to the tutor,
   'Is it harder to toot, or
To tutor two tooters to toot?'

Carolyn Wells

Simple Simon

Simple Simon met a pieman,
Going to the fair;
Says Simple Simon to the pieman,
'Let me taste your ware.'

Says the pieman to Simple Simon,
'Show me first your penny.'
Says Simple Simon to the pieman,
'Indeed I have not any.'

Simple Simon went a-fishing
For to catch a whale;
All the water he could find
Was in his mother's pail!

Simple Simon went to look
If plums grew on a thistle;
He pricked his fingers very much,
Which made poor Simon whistle.

He went to catch a dickey bird,
And thought he could not fail,
Because he had a little salt,
To put upon its tail.

He went for water with a sieve,
But soon it ran all through;
And now poor Simple Simon
Bids you all adieu.

Anon.

A Baby Sardine

A baby sardine
Saw her first submarine;
She was scared and watched through a peephole.

'Oh, come, come, come,'
Said the sardine's mum,
'It's only a tin full of people.'

Spike Milligan

Basil

When Cousin Basil
Played his bassoon
His body blew up
Like a barrage balloon

When I asked him shouldn't
He suck not blow
He swiftly answered
NOOOOOOOOOOOOOOOOOOOOOOOOOOOOOOOOOO
OOOOOOOOOOOOOOOOOOOOOOOOOOOOOOOOOO
OOOOOOOOOOOOOOOOOOOOOOOOOOOOOOOOO
OOOOOOOOOOOOOOOOOOOOOOOOOOOOOOOO
OOOOOOOOOOOOOOOOOOOOOOOO
OOOOOOOOOOOOOOOO
OOOOOOOO
OOOO
OO
O
  O
    O
     O
      O
       O
        O
         O
          O

Gareth Owen

Way Down South Where Bananas Grow

Way down south where bananas grow,
A grasshopper stepped on an elephant's toe.
The elephant said, with tears in his eyes,
'Pick on somebody your own size.'

Anon.

The Parent

Children aren't happy with nothing to ignore,
And that's what parents were created for.

Ogden Nash

13

In Trouble Again

Will you PLEASE
stop sniffing and blow your nose
tidy your things away
and hang up your clothes!
Please do something useful
like cleaning the hamster's cage
but most of all, Dad,
PLEASE just act your age!

Susan Quinn

Saint Valentine's Day Massacre

What did I ever do to Dorothy Prewitt?
She's sent me a heart with an arrow right through it!
So . . . if she wants war (well I didn't begin it)
I'll draw her a heart with an axe buried in it!

Philip Waddell

15

Fishing

There is a fine
line

between fishing
and standing
on the bank
like an idiot.

Gerard Benson

16

Little Boys

What are little boys made of?
    Frogs and snails
    And puppy-dogs' tails
That's what little boys are made of.

Anon.

17

Nobody Loves Me

Nobody loves me,
Everybody hates me,
I think I'll go and eat worms.

Big fat squishy ones,
Little thin skinny ones,
See how they wriggle and squirm.

Bite their heads off.
'Schlurp!' they're lovely,
Throw their tails away.

Nobody knows
How big I grows
On worms three times a day.

Anon.

18

No Peas for the Wicked

No peas for the wicked
No carrots for the damned
No parsnips for the naughty
  O Lord we pray

No sprouts for the shameless
No cabbage for the shady
No lettuce for the lecherous
  No way, no way

No potatoes for the deviants
No radish for the riff-raff
No spinach for the spineless
  Lock them away

No beetroot for the boasters
No mangetout for the mobsters
No corn-on-the-cob et cetera
  (Shall we call it a day?)

Roger McGough

She Likes to Swim Beneath the Sea

She likes to swim beneath the sea
And wear her rubber flippers,
She likes to dance outrageously
And wake up all the kippers.

Colin West

Not Funny

A sad old wizard waved his wand,
'Something to make me laugh,' he said.
A joke-book hurtled through the door
And bashed him on the head.

Mike Jubb

21

Dick's Dog

Dick had a dog
The dog dug
The dog dug deep
How deep did Dick's dog dig?

Dick had a duck
The duck dived
The duck dived deep
How deep did Dick's duck dive?

Dick's duck dived as deep as Dick's dog dug.

Trevor Millum

Three Wise Men of Gotham

Three wise men of Gotham
Went to sea in a bowl,
If the bowl had been stronger
My song had been longer.

Anon.

I'm Carrying the Baby

Paul was three.
'Look at me,' he said,
'look at me
I'm carrying the baby.
Look at me
look at me
I'm carrying the baby.'

'Oh,' said Paul,
'look at me
I've dropped the baby.'

Michael Rosen

Eletelephony

Once there was an elephant,
Who tried to use the telephant –
No! no! I mean an elephone
Who tried to use the telephone –
(Dear me! I am not certain quite
That even now I've got it right.)

Howe'er it was, he got his trunk
Entangled in the telephunk;
The more he tried to get it free,
The louder buzzed the telephee –
(I fear I'd better drop the song
Of elephop and telephong!)

Laura E. Richards

Oh, Ozzie!

'Polar bear in the garden!' yelled Ozzie,
And we all rushed out to see,
But of course it wasn't a bear at all –
Just a marmalade cat who'd jumped over the wall.
Oh, Ozzie!

'Mountain lion in the garden!' yelled Ozzie,
And we all rushed out to see,
But of course it wasn't a lion with a roar –
Just the scruffy black dog who'd dug in from next door.
Oh, Ozzie!

'Kangaroo in the garden!' yelled Ozzie,
And we all stayed in and smiled,
And of course it wasn't a kangaroo –
But a man-eating tiger escaped from the zoo.
Poor Ozzie.

Richard Edwards

26

Tring

There was an old lady from Tring
Who replied when they asked her to sing
  'You may find it odd
  But I cannot tell *God*
Save the Weasel from *Pop Goes the King.*'

Anon.

An Interesting Fact about One of My Relatives

M_y

great great great great
great great great great
great great great great
great great great great
great great great great
great great great great
great great great great

grandad is very old.

Ian McMillan

Gnomic

I am the oldest known gnome,
No gnome is older than me,
I am the oldest known gnome
Though an unknown gnome there may be.

An unknown gnome there may be
But nobody knows of him yet
Therefore no gnome is older than me
So give me a little respect.

John Mole

Crocodile

I met a crocodile today
I took it home with me
I introduced him to my folks
Who said, 'Please stay for tea.'

He didn't like the beans on toast
He didn't like the bread
But he liked my Aunt Gertrude
So he swallowed her instead.

Gareth Owen

March

Beautiful Soup

Beautiful Soup, so rich and green,
  Waiting in a hot tureen!
Who for such dainties would not stoop?
Soup of the evening, beautiful Soup!
Soup of the evening, beautiful Soup!
  Beau-ootiful Soo-oop!
  Beau-ootiful Soo-oop!
Soo-oop of the e-e-evening,
  Beautiful, beautiful Soup!

Beautiful Soup! Who cares for fish,
   Game, or any other dish?
Who would not give all else for two p
ennyworth only of beautiful Soup?
Pennyworth only of beautiful Soup?
   Beau-ootiful Soo-oop!
   Beau-ootiful Soo-oop!
Soo-oop of the e-e-evening,
   Beautiful, beauti-FUL SOUP!

Lewis Carroll

2

The Adventures of Isabel

Isabel met an enormous bear,
Isabel, Isabel, didn't care;
The bear was hungry, the bear was ravenous,
The bear's big mouth was cruel and cavernous.
The bear said, Isabel, glad to meet you,
How do, Isabel, now I'll eat you!
Isabel, Isabel, didn't worry,
Isabel didn't scream or scurry,
She washed her hands and she straightened her hair up,
Then Isabel quietly ate the bear up.

Once in a night as black as pitch
Isabel met a wicked witch.
The witch's face was cross and wrinkled,
The witch's gums with teeth were sprinkled.
Ho ho, Isabel! the old witch crowed,
I'll turn you into an ugly toad!
Isabel, Isabel, didn't worry,
Isabel didn't scream or scurry,
She showed no rage, she showed no rancour,
But she turned the witch into milk and drank her.

Isabel met a hideous giant,
Isabel continued self-reliant.
The giant was hairy, the giant was horrid,
He had one eye in the middle of his forehead.
Good morning, Isabel, the giant said,
I'll grind your bones to make my bread.
Isabel, Isabel, didn't worry,
Isabel didn't scream or scurry.
She nibbled the zwieback that she always fed off,
And when it was gone, she cut the giant's head off.

Isabel met a troublesome doctor,
He punched and he poked till he really shocked her.
The doctor's talk was of coughs and chills
And the doctor's satchel bulged with pills.
The doctor said unto Isabel,
Swallow this, it will make you well.
Isabel, Isabel, didn't worry,
Isabel didn't scream or scurry.
She took those pills from the pill concoctor,
And Isabel calmly cured the doctor.

Isabel once was asleep in bed
When a horrible dream crawled into her head.
It was worse than a dinosaur, worse than a shark,
Worse than an octopus oozing in the dark.
'Boo!' said the dream, with a dreadful grin,
'I'm going to scare you out of your skin!'
Isabel, Isabel, didn't worry,
Isabel didn't scream or scurry,
Isabel had a cleverer scheme;
She just woke up and fooled that dream.

Whenever you meet a bugaboo
Remember what Isabel used to do.
Don't scream when the bugaboo says 'Boo!'
Just look it in the eye and say, 'Boo to you!'
That's how to banish a bugaboo;
Isabel did it and so can you!
Boooooo to you.

Ogden Nash

I Built a Fabulous Machine

I built a fabulous machine
to keep my room completely clean.
It swept it up in nothing flat –
has anybody seen the cat?

Jack Prelutsky

4

The School for Spring

My first teaching job
was at the School for Spring

For years I worked there
teaching lambs to jump,
teaching buds how to open
and flowers to bloom.

By careful tuition
I trained the sun
to get up a little earlier each day.

I taught the cold hard rain
to be gentler
and warmer.

Daffodils,
crocuses
and cherry blossom
were my star pupils.

In my classes
even hibernating hedgehogs
would wake;
swallows travel
thousands of miles
to be there;
rare natterjack toads
would gather
and sing.

Nice for the while;
but such froth and fun
is not the stuff
of a lifelong career.

My new job
pays much better
and my classes are more solemn,
now I'm working
as a tutor
for the College of Autumn.

David Bateman

5

Matilda
who told lies, and was burned to death

Matilda told such Dreadful Lies,
It made one Gasp and Stretch one's Eyes;
Her Aunt, who, from her Earliest Youth,
Had kept a Strict Regard for Truth,
Attempted to Believe Matilda:
The effort very nearly killed her,
And would have done so, had not She
Discovered this Infirmity.
For once, towards the Close of Day,
Matilda, growing tired of play,
And finding she was left alone,
Went tiptoe to the Telephone
And summoned the Immediate Aid
Of London's Noble Fire-Brigade.
Within an hour the Gallant Band
Were pouring in on every hand,
From Putney, Hackney Downs and Bow,
With Courage high and Hearts a-glow
They galloped, roaring through the Town,
'Matilda's House is Burning Down!'
Inspired by British Cheers and Loud
Proceeding from the Frenzied Crowd,

They ran their ladders through a score
Of windows on the Ball Room Floor;
And took Peculiar Pains to Souse
The Pictures up and down the House,
Until Matilda's Aunt succeeded
In showing them they were not needed
And even then she had to pay
To get the Men to go away!

It happened that a few Weeks later
Her Aunt was off to the Theatre
To see that Interesting Play
The Second Mrs Tanqueray.
She had refused to take her Niece
To hear this Entertaining Piece:
A Deprivation Just and Wise
To Punish her for Telling Lies.
That Night a Fire *did* break out –
You should have heard Matilda Shout!
You should have heard her Scream and Bawl,
And throw the window up and call
To People passing in the Street –
(The rapidly increasing Heat
Encouraging her to obtain
Their confidence) – but all in vain!
For every time She shouted 'Fire!'
They only answered 'Little Liar!'
And therefore when her Aunt returned,
Matilda, and the House, were Burned.

Hilaire Belloc

6

Auntie's Boyfriend
(for Brian and Lu, with love)

Auntie's brought her boyfriend home. He's sitting in a chair.
He wears an ear-ring and he's got no hair.

He's crazy about football and I'm glad about that.
He's polite to my Granny, he's kind to the cat
But I have to make an effort not to stand and stare
Cos he wears an ear-ring and he's got no hair.

He eats his dinner nicely. His manners are OK.
He sips his tea in silence in an ordinary way.
He nibbles with decorum at a chocolate éclair –
But he wears an ear-ring and he's got no hair.

I'll ring up the gang. I'll ring them for a dare:
'Come round this evening, there's a secret I must share.
Auntie's brought her boyfriend home. He's sitting in a chair
And he wears an ear-ring and he's got no hair.'

Fred Sedgwick

Haircut Rap

Ah sey, ah want it short,
Short back an' side,
Ah tell him man, ah tell him
When ah teck him aside,
Ah sey, ah want a haircut
Ah can wear with pride,
So lef' it long on top
But short back an' side.

Ah sey try an' put a pattern
In the shorter part,
Yuh could put a skull an' crossbone,
Or an arrow through a heart,
Meck sure ah have enough hair lef'
Fe cover me wart,
Lef' a likkle pon the top,
But the res' – keep it short.

Well, bwoy, him start to cut
An' me settle down to wait,
Him was cuttin' from seven
Till half-past eight,
Ah was startin' to get worried
'Cause ah see it gettin' late,
But then him put the scissors down
Sey, 'There yuh are, mate.'

Well ah did see a skull an' a
Criss-cross bone or two,
But was me own skull an' bone
That was peepin' through
Ah look jus' like a monkey
Ah did see once at the zoo,
Him say, 'What's de matter, Tammy,
Don't yuh like the hair-do?'

Well, ah feel me heart stop beatin'
When ah look pon me reflection,
Ah feel like somet'ing frizzle up
Right in me middle section
Ah look aroun' fe somewhey
Ah could crawl into an' hide
The day ah mek me brother cut
Me hair short back an' side.

Valerie Bloom

Junk Uncle

Bless Uncle Bert, untidy twit
So fond of trash, he lived in it,
In love with litter, master of mess,
How did he end up? Have a guess!
Picked up by the rubbish man,
Chucked in the back of the refuse van,
Uncle Bert, to dirt attracted,
Ended his days somewhat compacted.

Andrew Fusek Peters

Government Health Warning

Don't squash peas on your knees,
Don't grate carrot on a parrot,
Don't tangle pears in your nostril hairs
Never risk a quid on a squid.

Don't pour bottled beer in your ear.
Never slice apple pies on your thighs.
Never wash your pullovers with yesterday's leftovers.
Don't entice a bowl of egg fried rice.

Don't assume that tarragon's a paragon,
Or try to run faster than a bag of spinach pasta,
Don't try to lunge at Victoria sponge,
A cake with a steak is a mistake.

Bravado never works with avocado,
A flickin's not the thing to give to chicken,
Don't go and stutter on the b-b-b-b-butter
Never feed mice on ice.

Careful not to ravage a coy savoy cabbage,
Never have a tussle with a mussel,
Don't ever hurry with a spicy prawn curry,
Don't boast about your buttered toast.

Don't pour jelly in your welly,
Don't dribble tagliatelle on your older brother's belly.
Never do the tango with a ripe and juicy mango,
If you do then you're sure to pay the price!

Chrissie Gittins

Next!

I thought that I would like to see
The early world that used to be.
That mastodonic mausoleum,
The Natural History Museum.
At midnight in the vasty hall
The fossils gathered for a ball.
High above notices and bulletins
Loomed up the Mesozoic skeletons.
Aroused by who knows what elixirs,
They ground along like concrete mixers.
They bowed and scraped in reptile pleasure,
And then began to tread the measure.
There were no drums or saxophones,
But just the clatter of their bones,
A rolling, rattling carefree circus
Of mammoth polkas and mazurkas.
Pterodactyls and brontosauruses
Sang ghostly prehistoric choruses.
Amid the megalosauric wassail
I caught the eye of one small fossil.
Cheer up, old man, he said, and winked –
It's kind of fun to be extinct.

Ogden Nash

11

We All Have to Go

The sound drew nearer;
a wheezy, hoarse breathing
as if some heavy weight
were being dragged along.
There was a smell of burnt bones.
A horny, hairy finger edged
round the trickling, slimy wall.
Then a large warty nose,
topped by bloodshot watery eyes,
Slowly emerged from the gloom.
The eyes widened, glowing
to a bright red.
Its pace quickened and soon
it towered above us.
The huge slavering mouth opened –
'Any of you lot know where
the toilet is?'

John C. Desmond

Fruit Jokes

The Satsuma
Has no sense of humour
But a fig'll
Giggle

Adrian Mitchell

13

The Great Panjandrum

So she went into the garden
to cut a cabbage-leaf
to make an apple pie;
and at the same time
a great she-bear, coming down the street,
pops its head into the shop.
What! no soap?
    So he died,
and she very imprudently married the Barber:
and there were present

the Picninnies,
    and the Joblillies,
        and the Garyulies,
and the great Panjandrum himself,
with the little round button at top;
and they all fell to playing the game of catch-as-catch-can
till the gunpowder ran out at the heels of their boots.

Samuel Foote

Elizabeth I

Elizabeth the First, I hear,
Was quite a fussy queen,
And had a hot bath once a year
To keep her body clean.

Colin West

Georgie Porgie

Georgie Porgie, pudding and pie,
Kissed the girls and made them cry;
When the boys came out to play,
Georgie Porgie ran away.

Anon.

16

Instructions for Giants

Please do not step on swing parks, youth clubs,
   cinemas or skate parks.
Please flatten all schools!

Please do not eat children, pop stars, TV soap actors,
   kind grannies who give us 50p.
Please feel free to gobble up dentists and teachers
   any time you like!

Please do not block out the sunshine.
Please push all rain clouds over to France.

Please do not drink the public swimming pool.
Please eat all cabbage fields, vegetable plots
   and anything green that grows in the
      boring countryside!

Please do not trample kittens, lambs or other baby animals.
Please take spiders and snakes, ants and beetles home
   for your pets.

March

Please stand clear of jets passing.
Please sew up the ozone layer.
Please mind where you're putting your big feet –
and no sneaking off to China when we're playing
hide-and-seek!

John Rice

17

My Baby Brother's Secrets

When my baby brother
wants to tell me a secret,
he comes right up close.
But instead of putting his lips
against my ear,
he presses his ear
tightly against my ear.
Then, he whispers so softly
that I can't hear
a word he is saying.

My baby brother's secrets
are safe with me.

John Foster

Literacy Hour

So let's make this clear,
An ADJECTIVE is a
DESCRIBING WORD . . .
(The long, winding, deep, dark, gloomy, secret
Tunnel leads under
The cold, bare, windy, wet, empty
Playground to the
Wild, wonderful, sunny, exciting, outside
World.)

And a NOUN, of course,
Is an OBJECT, a SUBJECT,
A THING . . .
(If only I had
A glider, or a private jet, or a space rocket,
    or a hot-air balloon, or a time machine,
I could fly away to
The seaside, or the zoo, or a forest, or Egypt,
    or Disneyland, or Anywhere-But-Here.)

A VERB, as we all know,
I hope,
Is a DOING WORD . . .
(I could run, or race, or tiptoe, or clamber,
    or catapult, or dance, or whirl, or just walk
My way to freedom.)

And an ADVERB tells you
Exactly how the action
Is done . . .
(Joyfully, happily, noisily, silently, timidly,
    bravely, desperately, frantically, urgently,
        nervously, wistfully, longingly, dreamily,
Someday,
Sometime,
Soon.)

Clare Bevan

Four Seasons

Spring is showery, flowery, bowery.
Summer: hoppy, choppy, poppy.
Autumn: wheezy, sneezy, freezy.
Winter: slippy, drippy, nippy.

Anon.

Ladles and Jellyspoons

Ladles and Jellyspoons,
I come before you
To stand behind you
And tell you something
I know nothing about.
Next Thursday
Which is Good Friday

There'll be a Mothers' Meeting
For Fathers only.
Wear your best clothes if you haven't any
And if you can come
Please stay at home.
Admission free
Pay at the door
Take a seat
And sit on the floor.
It makes no difference where you sit
The man in the gallery is sure to spit.

Anon.

21

The Mysteries of Nature
(or Globular Bunkular My Duck Has Sunkular)

Nature poems are popular
    but seldom very jocular
But this one is spectacular
    because it's quite funicular

Let's take a country walkular
through fields that are rusticular
look through your binocular
there's an eagle and a hawkular

The hedgerow in particular
is a home so very insular
for creatures shaped triangular
or even semi-circular

You may come across a spookular
in the forest deep and darkular
a sharp stab in your jugular
means you've met up with Count Dracular

By the church that looks so secular
there is a pond where you'll find a duckular
this one doesn't quackular
since it argued with a truckular

I see by the town clockular
that time is passing quickular
I think I need a breakular
too much nature makes you sickular

John Rice

Shoe, Boot! Shoe!

Dear Shoe, I've got
a crush on you,
I think you're
b-o-o-t-i-f-u-l.
Please, could you take a
shine to me or do you find me dull?
Dear Boot, you are a silly clog so kindly hold your tongue.
You are a heel and my soft soul, by you, will not be won.
Boot felt his throat tie in a knot. Shoe'd walked all over him!
And now he's stashed back on the shelf,
alone,   out on a limb.

Gina Douthwaite

23

The Lone Teacher

We've got a new teacher
he wears a mask
and a big wide hat.

He comes to school
on a silver horse
and rides around the field
all day.

Sometimes he says,
'Have you seen Toronto?'

We tell him
we haven't been to Canada
but is it near
the Panama Canal
we did that in geography
last term?

At four o'clock
he rides off into the sunset
and comes back the next morning
in a cloud of dust.

We wonder if
he will ever come and teach us maths
like he said he would
when he first arrived.

Perhaps then he'll tell us his name
not keep it a secret
because my dad always asks me,
'Who is that man?'

David Harmer

Batgirl's Disgrace

Auntie Betty pulls her cloak on
And the mask – the one with ears.
Then she flies out of the classroom
Fighting back a flood of tears
All the teachers in the playground
Wag their fingers at the girl
If only she had done her homework
First, before she saved the world

Need calamity prevention?
Sorry. Batgirl's in detention

Andrea Shavick

25

On the Ning Nang Nong

On the Ning Nang Nong
Where the Cows go Bong!
And the Monkeys all say Boo!
There's a Nong Nang Ning
Where the trees go Ping!
And the tea pots Jibber Jabber Joo.
On the Nong Ning Nang
All the mice go Clang!
And you just can't catch 'em when they do!
So it's Ning Nang Nong!
Cows go Bong!
Nong Nang Ning!
Trees go Ping!
Nong Ning Nang!
The mice go Clang!
What a noisy place to belong,
Is the Ning Nang Ning Nang Nong!!

Spike Milligan

Taking My Human for a Walk

I took my human for a walk
Along the beach

The fishing nets had dragged in
Hundreds of spider crabs
Dead and rotting on the shingle
I rolled and rolled in them
Sheer bliss

When we got home
I nearly died of embarrassment
My human said,
'Look, you have a crab's claw
stuck to your tail.'

Roger Stevens

27

Do We Have to Kiss?

Do we have to Kiss?
Can't we just hold hands
Can't we both agree
To make other plans?
I might accidentally get your nose
Get the giggles
If I tread on your toes
A hand-shake won't do instead, I suppose?
Do we have to Kiss?

Do we have to Kiss?
Are we old enough
Do we need this wet, romantic stuff
Are you sure that you know what to do
Should I stand on your chair
Cos I'm shorter than you
Do we have to Kiss?

Do we have to Kiss?
Do you think it's true
That it gives you spots and gastric flu
Makes your jaw-bone ache
And your ears turn pink
Isn't it just like plunging
A blocked-up sink
Do we have to Kiss?

If we're going to Kiss
Better do it quick
The anticipation makes me sick
. . . It's not too bad
It's almost fun
Now slowly
Give me another one . . .

Lindsay MacRae

28

Seven Solemn and Serious
Superstitions

If you're at the supermarket
and your trolley wheels get stuck
it means your head will soon fall off
not the best of luck!

If you walk beneath a bridge
some man is painting green
you'll turn into a Brussels sprout,
perhaps a runner bean.

If you sneeze when you're at school
stick a carrot in your ear
flip a cartwheel and shout 'PANTS!'
or else you'll disappear.

If you drop a pile of plates
upon the kitchen floor
throw bags of salt at your Mum
or be cursed for evermore.

If your lessons get you down
to have a better time
write five rude words upon the board
and make sure that they rhyme.

If three brown dogs and five white cats
are dancing down your road
rub your head with engine oil
or else you will explode!

If you want good luck all week
stuff mustard up your nose
keep a bright green clover leaf
between your little toes.

All these sayings will come true
and help in every way
believe them all through thick and thin
whatever people say.

David Harmer

29

Lines by a Humanitarian

Be lenient to lobsters, and ever kind to crabs,
And be not disrespectful to cuttlefish or dabs;

Chase on the Cochin-China, chaff not the ox obese
And babble not of feather-beds in company with geese.

Be tender with the tadpole, and let the limpet thrive,
Be merciful to mussels, don't skin your eels alive;

When talking to a turtle, don't mention calipee –
Be always kind to animals wherever you may be.

Anon.

30

It Wasn't Me

It wasn't me, sir, honest, sir.
It wasn't me, sir, it was him.
I wasn't with him, honest, sir.
It was definitely him, sir,
but I definitely wasn't with him, honest, sir.
Honest, sir, I'm telling the truth,
it wasn't me, it was him, sir.
It can't have been me, sir,
I wasn't with him.
Honest, sir.

I was quite near him though.

Paul Cookson

31

Antelopes

Now there's a headline.
You fill in the blanks:
Beetle loves Ant.
Ant loves Beetle.
But their parents don't approve.
Beetle puts a ladder up against the ant hill.
Ant runs down.
Ant elopes.

Philip Ardagh

April

April the First

One Literacy Hour
Our teacher, Miss Telling,
Said, 'Write down these words.
I am testing your spelling.'

1. Aardvark.
2. Proboscis.
3. Rhododendron.
4. Iridescent.
5. Lexicographer.
6. Fahrenheit.
7. Orchid
8. Onomatopoeia.
9. Llanfairpwllgwyngyllgogerychwyrndrobwllllantysiliogo-
   gogoch.

But when we all groaned
And we all cursed our fate,
Miss Telling just smiled
And said, 'Now add the date.'

Clare Bevan

A Tree Toad Loved a She-toad

A tree toad loved a she-toad
    That lived up a tree.
She was a three-toed tree toad
    But a two-toed toad was he.
The two-toed toad tried to win
    The she-toad's friendly nod,
For the two-toed toad loved the ground
    On which the three-toed toad trod.
But no matter how the two-toed tree toad tried,
    He could not please her whim.
In her tree-toad bower,
    With her three-toed power
The she-toad vetoed him.

Anon.

3

Match of the Year

I am delivered to the stadium by chauffeur-driven limousine.
Gran and Grandpa give me a lift in their Mini.

I change into my sparkling clean world-famous designer strip.
*I put on my brother's shorts and the T-shirt with tomato
ketchup stains.*

I give my lightweight professional boots a final shine.
I rub the mud off my trainers.

The coach gives me a final word of encouragement.
Dave, the sports master, tells me to get a move on.

I jog calmly through the tunnel into the stadium.
I walk nervously on to the windy sports field.

The crowd roars.
Gran and Grandpa shout, 'There's our Jimmy!'

The captain talks last-minute tactics.
'Pass to me or I'll belt you.'

The whistle goes. The well-oiled machine goes into action.
Where did the ball go?

I pass it skilfully to our international star, Bernicci.
*I kick it away. Luckily, Big Bernard stops it before it goes
   over the line.*

A free kick is awarded to the visiting Premier team. I'm part
   of the impregnable defence.
*The bloke taking the kick looks six feet tall – and just as
   wide . . .*

I stop the ball with a well-timed leap and head it expertly up
   the field.
The ball thwacks me on the head.

The crowd shouts my name! 'Jim-meee! Jim-meee! Jim-meee!'
Gran says, 'Eee, our Jim's fallen over.'

   I don't remember any more.

Trevor Millum

A Centipede

A centipede was happy quite,
Until a frog in fun
Said, 'Pray which leg comes after which?'
This raised her mind to such a pitch
She lay distracted in a ditch
Considering how to run.

Anon.

On the Pavement

Sauntering along alone I hear other busier footsteps behind me.
Not feeling threatened but awkward
I wonder, should I slow down my walking
and let them get by as soon as possible
or shall I imperceptibly quicken to a higher gear
before they are near enough to notice?
Ah, it's OK, it sounds like they've just fallen over.

John Hegley

Mary Had a Crocodile

Mary had a crocodile
That ate a child each day,
But interfering people came
And took her pet away.

Anon.

Different Ways to Put Up Your Hand in Lessons

Some stay silent
Arms straight up;
Some pretend –
A cover-up.

Some wave fingers,
Some stay still,
Some salute and
Some windmill.

Some fearless kids
Wave and click.
Some go upright
With a flick.

Some kids' hands
Are acrobatic.
Others wave
On automatic.

One or two
Are quite fantastic,
Wobbly hands
Made of elastic.

Some at angles
Dare to whistle;
Make their teacher's
Hackles bristle.

Others like to
Moan and groan
As if the answer
was well-known.

And one or two
Say not a word –
For what was asked
They never heard.

Pie Corbett

The Shark

A treacherous monster is the Shark
He never makes the least remark.

And when he sees you on the sand,
He doesn't seem to want to land.

He watches you take off your clothes,
And not the least excitement shows.

His eyes do not grow bright or roll,
He has astounding self-control.

He waits till you are quite undrest,
And seems to take no interest.

And when towards the sea you leap,
He looks as if he were asleep.

But when you once get in his range,
His whole demeanour seems to change.

He throws his body right about,
And his true character comes out.

It's no use crying or appealing,
He seems to lose all decent feeling.

After this warning you will wish
To keep clear of this treacherous fish.

His back is black, his stomach white,
He has a very dangerous bite.

Lord Alfred Douglas

What For?

One more word, said my dad,
And I'll give you what for.

What for? I said.

That's right, he said, what for!

No, I said, I mean what for?
What will you give me what for for?

Never you mind, he said. Wait and see.

But what is what for for? I said.

What's what for for? he said.
It's to teach you what's what,
That's what.

What's that? I said.

Right, he said, you're for it,
I'm going to let you have it.

Have what? I said.

Have what? he said,
What for, that's what.
Do you want me to really give you
Something to think about?

I don't know, I said,
I'm thinking about it.

Then he clipped me over the ear.

It was the first time he'd made sense
All day.

Noel Petty

10

Introducing Dad

If I may, Miss
I'd like to introduce my dad
Mum left us last year
And that made him really sad
He told me you were pretty
And his favourite colour's beige
And it isn't uncommon
To date women half your age
And we all know that he's bald
Beneath that funny flick of hair
You just have to humour him
And pretend his hair's all there
His feet smell a bit funny
And his brain's a trifle slow
And you haven't got a boyfriend, Miss
So . . . could you please give Dad a go?

Roger Stevens

11

No Bread

I wish I'd made a list,
I forgot to get the bread.
If I forget it again
I'll be dead.

We had blank and butter pudding,
beans on zip.
Boiled eggs with deserters,
no chip butty: just chip.

I wish I'd made a list,
I forgot to get the bread.
My mam got the empty bread bin
and wrapped it round my head.

Our jam sarnies were just jam
floating in the air.
We spread butter on the table
cos the bread wasn't there.

My mam says if I run away
she knows I won't be missed,
not like the bread was . . .
I wish I'd made a list!

Ian McMillan

Interrogation in the Nursery

Infant: What's that?
Inspector: What?
Infant: That on your face.
Inspector: It's a moustache.
Infant: What does it do?
Inspector: It doesn't do anything.
Infant: Oh.
Inspector: It just sits there on my lip.
Infant: Does it go up your nose?
Inspector: No.
Infant: Could I stroke it?
Inspector: No.
Infant: Is it alive?
Inspector: No, it's not alive.

Infant: Can I have one?
Inspector: *No, little girls don't have moustaches.*
Infant: Why?
Inspector: *Well, they just don't.*
Infant: Can I have one when I grow up?
Inspector: *No, ladies don't have moustaches either.*
Infant: Well my granny's got one!

Gervase Phinn

The Smiling Villain

Forth from his den to steal he stole,
His bags of chink he chunk,
And many a wicked smile he smole,
And many a wink he wunk.

Anon.

Daddy Fell into the Pond

Everyone grumbled. The sky was grey.
We had nothing to do and nothing to say.
We were nearing the end of a dismal day.
And there seemed to be nothing beyond,
   Then
      Daddy fell into the pond!

And everyone's face grew merry and bright,
And Timothy danced for sheer delight.
'Give me the camera, quick, oh quick!
He's crawling out of the duckweed!' Click!

Then the gardener suddenly slapped his knee,
And doubled up, shaking silently,
And the ducks all quacked as if they were daft,
And it sounded as if the old drake laughed.
Oh, there wasn't a thing that didn't respond
   When
      Daddy fell into the pond!

Alfred Noyes

15

There Once Was a Man

There once was a man
Called Knocketty Ned
Who wore his cat
On top of his head.
Upstairs, downstairs,
The whole world knew
Wherever he went
The cat went too.

He wore it at work,
He wore it at play,
He wore it to town
On market day,
And for fear it should rain
Or the snowflakes fly
He carried a brolly
To keep it dry.

He never did fret
Nor fume because
He always knew
Just where it was.
'And when,' said Ned,
'In my bed I lie
There's no better nightcap
Money can buy.

'There's no better bonnet
To be found,'
Said Knocketty Ned,
'The world around.
And furthermore
Was there ever a hat
As scared a mouse
Or scared a rat?'

Did you ever hear
Of a tale like that
As Knocketty Ned's
And the tale of his cat?

Charles Causley

16

School Dinners

If you stay to school dinners
Better throw them aside.
A lot of kids didn't,
A lot of kids died.
The meat is of iron,
The puds are of steel.
If the gravy don't get you,
The custard will.

Anon.

The Dark Avenger

My dog is called The Dark Avenger
Hello, I'm Cuddles

She understands every word I say
Woof?

Last night I took her for a walk
Woof! Walkies! Let's go!

Cleverly, she kept three paces ahead
I dragged him along behind me

She paused at every danger, spying out the land
I stopped at every lamp-post

When the coast was clear, she sped on
I slipped my lead and ran away

Scenting danger, Avenger investigated
I found some fresh chip papers in the bushes

I followed, every sense alert
*He blundered through the trees, shouting 'Oy, Come 'ere!
  Where are you?'*

Something – maybe a sixth sense – told me to stop
He tripped over me in the dark

There was a pale menacing figure ahead of us
Then I saw the white Scottie from next door

Avenger sprang into battle, eager to defend his master
Never could stand terriers

They fought like tigers
We scrapped like dogs

Until the enemy was defeated
Till Scottie's owner pulled him off – spoilsport!

Avenger gave a victory salute
I rolled in the puddles

And came to check I was all right
I shook mud over him

'Stop it, you stupid dog!'
He congratulated me

Sometimes, even The Dark Avenger can go too far.
Woof!

Trevor Millum

The Firefly

The firefly is a funny bug,
He hasn't any mind;
He blunders all the way through life
With his headlight on behind.

Anon.

The Way to the Zoo

That's the way to the zoo.
That's the way to the zoo.
The monkey house is nearly full
But there's room enough for you.

Anon.

20

Why?

Why does Mum look so furtive
when I ask her where she has been?
Why does she keep an old sea chest
and what does her parrot mean
when it squawks out, 'Shiver me timbers'
and 'Bring out those pieces of eight'?
Why is Mum always phoning
someone she calls the first mate,
why does she peel the potatoes
with a cutlass, a mean-looking tool
and why does she wear soggy seaboots
when she comes to collect me from school?

Then why does she keep on singing,
'Yo ho ho and a bottle of rum'
and wearing that silly black eyepatch?
It's not what one expects of a mum.
And why does she bury treasure
under the pear tree at night
and why does she sometimes look
as if she's been caught in a fight?
I just haven't found any answers;
in fact I keep drawing a blank
but I'll just ask this one last question,
why am I walking the plank?

Marian Swinger

21

Science Lesson

We've done 'Water' and 'Metals' and 'Plastic'.
Today, it's the turn of 'Elastic':
Sir sets up a test . . .
Wow, that was the best –
he whizzed through the window. Fantastic!

Mike Johnson

My Chat-up Technique Needs an MOT

During the fifteen-minute
gap between
Geography

and Maths

I asked Pamela Whitethorn
If she would like to go to the pictures.
'Yes.'
With me?
'No.'

Another case of
break failure.

John Coldwell

Today I saw a little worm

Today I saw a little worm
Wriggling on his belly.
Perhaps he'd like to come inside
And see what's on the Telly.

Spike Milligan

The Dog

The truth I do not stretch or shove
When I state the dog is full of love.
I've also proved, by actual test,
A wet dog is the lovingest.

Ogden Nash

I Eat My Peas with Honey

I eat my peas with honey,
I've done it all my life.
It makes the peas taste funny,
But it keeps them on the knife.

Anon.

26

Hello, Mrs Morley

Hello, Mrs Morley, as you can see
There's nobody home now apart from me.
And I can't ask you in for a nice cup of tea
Because Mummy is hiding behind the settee,
And she's not coming out – whatever I say –
Until she's quite sure that you've gone away.

One thing, Mrs Morley, before you go,
There's something I really would like to know –
Just what *is* a name-dropping, snooty-nosed cat?
Next door have a Siamese – is it like that?

Jan Dean

Hot Food

We sit down to eat
and the potato's a bit hot
so I only put a little bit on my fork
and I blow
whooph whooph
until it's cool
just cool
Then into the mouth
nice.
And there's my brother
he's doing the same
whooph whooph
into the mouth
nice.
There's my mum
she's doing the same
whooph whooph
into the mouth
nice.

But my dad.
My dad.
What does he do?
He stuffs a great big chunk of potato
into his mouth.
Then
that really does it.
His eyes pop out
he flaps his hands
he blows, he puffs, he yells
he bobs his head up and down
he spits bits of potato
all over his plate
and he turns to us and he says,
'Watch out, everybody –
the potato's very hot.'

Michael Rosen

Moses

Moses supposes his toeses are roses,
But Moses supposes erroneously;
For nobody's toeses are posies of roses
As Moses supposes his toeses to be.

Anon.

A Sticky Riddle

It might seem obvious to you humans

But it puzzles me every day

If he wants the stick so badly

Why does he throw it away?

Roger Stevens

30

The Baby-sitter

It was clear
From the moment
They walked out the door
That Tracey
Had never done
This job before.

Until they came home
She patiently sat
On me
      my little brother
            and the cat.

Lindsay MacRae

May

Aaaaargh!

My aunty folds my face up,
Squeezes it like a concertina
Between her bony hands.
Then puckers up her mouth
into a wet doughnut –
Comeherecomeherecomehere
She says. Though I'm already there
And I can't get away.
Comeherecomeherecomehere
And I see it –
A slow-mo doughnut moving
Unstoppable through the air.
And I know, I just know,
That when it lands,
This killer kiss
Will be A WET ONE.

Jan Dean

There was a young girl of Asturias

There was a young girl of Asturias
Whose temper was frantic and furious
She used to throw eggs
At her grandmother's legs –
A habit unpleasant and curious

Anon.

3

What the Head Teacher Said When He Saw Me Running Out of School at 1.15 p.m. on 21 July Last Year to Buy an Ice Cream from Pelozzi's Van

Hey!*

Fred Sedgwick

* This poem is an attempt on three world records at once: the longest title, the longest footnote and the shortest text of any poem in the western world. It has been lodged with the Guinness Book of Records.

Sandra Slater

Here lies what's left of Sandra Slater
Who poked her pet – an alligator –
Forgetting that to tease or bait her
Might annoy an alligator.

Alas, the alligator ate her.

John Foster

5

Before the Days of Noah

Before the days of Noah
before he built his ark
seagulls sang like nightingales
and lions sang like larks.
The tortoise had a mighty roar

the cockerel had a moo

kitten always eeyored

and elephants just mewed.
   It was the way the world was
   . . . when owls had a bark
   and dogs did awful crowings
   whilst running round the park.

Horses baaed like baa lambs
ducks could all miaow
and animals had voices
quite different from now!
But, came the day of flooding
and all the world was dark
the animals got weary
of living in the ark –
  So they swapped around their voices
  a trumpet for a mew
  – a silly sort of pastime
  when nothing much to do.
But when the flood had ended
and the world was nice and dry
the creatures had forgotten
how once they hissed or cried.

So they kept their brand-new voices
  – forgot the days before
  – when lions used to giggle
  and gerbils used to roar.

Peter Dixon

6

The Cod

There's something very strange and odd
About the habits of the Cod.

For when you're swimming in the sea,
He sometimes bites you on the knee.

And though his bites are not past healing,
It is a most unpleasant feeling.

And when you're diving down below,
He often nips you on the toe.

And though he doesn't hurt you much,
He has a disagreeable touch.

There's one thing to be said for him, –
It is a treat to see him swim.

But though he swims in graceful curves,
He rather gets upon your nerves.

Lord Alfred Douglas

149

Fear

I'd rather be caught by a python,
I'd rather be covered in fleas,
I'd rather be eaten by spiders
or boy-eating sharks in the seas.

I'd rather be chased by a monster,
melted alive by the sun,
eat bogies, and earwax forever, than:
be kissed in the playground by Mum.

Peter Dixon

Whoever Sausage a Thing?

One day a boy went walking
And went into a store;
He bought a pound of sausages
And laid them on the floor.

The boy began to whistle
A merry little tune –
And all the little sausages
Danced around the room.

Anon.

The Germ

A mighty creature is the germ,
Though smaller than the pachyderm.
His customary dwelling place
Is deep within the human race.
His childish pride he often pleases
By giving people strange diseases.
Do you, my poppet, feel infirm?
You probably contain a germ.

Ogden Nash

10

There Was a Young Lad of St Just

There was a young lad of St Just
Who ate apple pie till he bust.
  It wasn't the fru-it
  That caused him to do it,
What finished him off was the crust.

Anon.

11

Didn't He Dance!

Boy, didn't he dance that day!
Our teacher was whistling for the end of play
And after that penetrating peep
We were waiting for the second whistle
As still as sheep . . .
When he started a wild, mad, ranting dance
Beating and flapping with his hands at his pants.

It went on and on with him going berserk
All of a spasm and a twitch and a jerk.
Well, at last he stopped and whistled us in
And as we went past, with a sheepish grin
He said, 'Take no notice of that, I beg,
I'd just got a wasp up my trouser leg.'
Smart remark to him by my friend Sally:
'Nice one, sir! You should take up ballet.'

Eric Finney

I Raised a Great Hullabaloo

I raised a great hullabaloo
When I found a large mouse in my stew,
Said the waiter, 'Don't shout
And wave it about,
Or the rest will be wanting one, too!'

Anon.

153

The Thingy

Shin kicker
Snot flicker
Crisp muncher
Shoulder huncher
Grudge bearer
Out starer
Back stabber
Biscuit grabber
Sock smeller
Fib teller
Thinks that it's
Uri Geller.

Loud belcher
Slug squelcher
Pillow drooler
I'm the ruler
Gonna beat yer
That'll teach yer
Bog ugly
Swamp creature
Found mainly
Under-cover
What is it?

MY BROTHER!

Lindsay MacRae

14

Batman's Exercise Video

Pull on the tights
Yeah, pull on the tights
Pull up the trunks
Yeah, pull up the trunks

I said twirl the cape
        twirl the cape
        twirl the cape
        twirl the cape

Pull on the boots
Yeah, pull on the boots
Snap on the mask
Yeah, snap on the mask

I said twirl the cape
        twirl the cape
        twirl the cape
        twirl the cape

Repeat until opponents are fully dazzled . . .

Ian McMillan

15

I've Seen Mrs Newton's Knickers

You'll never believe what I've seen!
Go on . . . have a guess
I've seen Mrs Newton's knickers
The pairs she wears beneath her dress.

Monday's pair is navy blue and thick
Because she teaches Games.
Tuesday's Science so they're fireproof
From the Bunsen burner's flames.

Wednesday she has lots of pairs
To add and take or share in Maths.
Thursday's pair is waterproof
Because of swimming at the baths.

Friday's pair is vast, expansive,
Thermal, flannelette and so
Warming freezing playtime duties
They will reach from head to toe.

May

Wimbledon or tennis fortnight
Then they're white and rather frilly.
Do not look on April Fool's Day
Because they're very very silly.

Yellow spots, blue polka dots,
Tartan checks, deckchair stripes
But the most amazing pair
Is saved for raves on Saturday nights.

Black and silky, shiny satin,
Very elegant and lacy.
Very brief beyond belief
Rather risqué, really racy.

I've seen Mrs Newton's knickers
Every pattern, each design
Every style in every colour
Hung up on her washing line!

Paul Cookson

16

Hogging Hedgehogs
(With thanks to Lewis Carroll)

'Won't you trot a little faster?' said the hedgehog to the
cat,
'The slugs are sliming frothily, there are earwigs brown and
fat,
The snails are ripe for picking, there's a thousand grubs at
least,
They are lurking in the compost heap, won't you come and
join the feast?

*'Will you, won't you, will you, won't you, will you join the
feast?
Will you, won't you, will you, won't you, won't you join the
feast?*

'You really can't imagine how delightful it will taste
When we bite into a beetle, or a worm, so let's make haste!
When he thinks of hogging maggots a hedgehog almost runs,
For those that get there early get the fat and juicy ones!

'*Will you, won't you, will you, won't you, will you join the feast?*
Will you, won't you, will you, won't you, won't you join the feast?'

'I'm sure it sounds delicious,' his furry friend replied,
'So please enjoy your centipedes, with woodlice on the side,
But I've no need to join you, for I have a well trained man,
And when I'm feeling hungry, why, he'll open up a can!'

I will not, could not, will not, could not, will not join the feast!
I will not, could not, will not, could not, could not join the feast!

David Orme

17

The Ferret Poem

There's very little merit in a ferret
Whipping up your trouser leg
Very little merit in a ferret
Whipping up your trouser leg

If it were a pine marten
Oh boy you'd be smarting
If it were a puma you'd be dead.

There's very little merit in a ferret
Whipping up your trouser leg.

So if you dote on a stoat
If your heart goes blink for a mink
If you play footloose
With a mongoose
If you potter with an otter
If your beazel is a weasel
If your heart is set
On a marmoset
Then think

There's very little merit in a ferret
Whipping up your trouser leg

Ferrets, stoats, they are vermin
You don't want your underpants
Trimmed with ermine

There's very little merit in a ferret
Whipping up your trouser leg.

PS When I wrote this poem I made a mistake. I thought a
   marmoset was a type of ferret-like creature. It isn't. It's a
   small monkey. I meant a marmot . . . which of course is a
   small type of Bovril.

David Harmer

Algy Met a Bear

Algy met a Bear,
a bear met Algy:
the bear grew bulgy;
the bulge was Algy.

Anon.

Arthur, My Half-Cousin

One eye, one ear, one nostril
One arm, one leg, one hand
Arthur, my half-cousin
Is half the boy I am.

One knee, one foot, one ankle
I'm twelve, he's half a dozen
I'm twice the boy that Arthur is
Arthur – half a cousin.

Paul Cookson

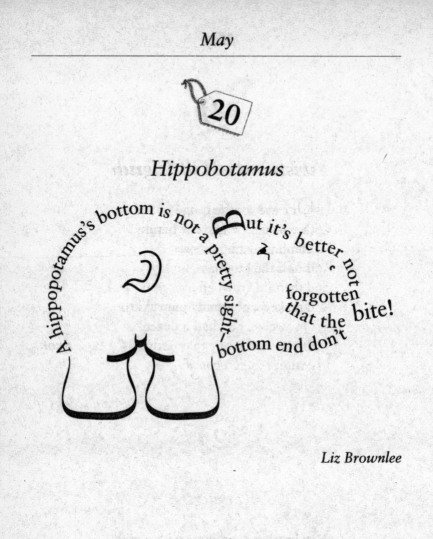

20

Hippobotamus

A hippopotamus's bottom is not a pretty sight— But it's better not forgotten that the bite! bottom end don't

Liz Brownlee

I wish I was a little grub

I wish I was a little grub
With whiskers round my tummy.
I'd climb into a honey-pot
And make my tummy gummy.
And then I'd crawl all over you
And make your tummy gummy, too.

Anon.

Revenge

My brother chased me with a crab,
He found it by a rock,
But I *will* get my own back –
It's now inside his sock!

Coral Rumble

A Visit to Yalding

We went to Yalding to look at the locks
To watch the water going up and down.
My brother found a dead sparrow to take home,
My mum found a ten pence piece,
My dad picked up a tin can that an animal might hurt itself
    on
And I –
I fell in the river.

I dripped back to the car.
'You're not getting into the car like that,'
said Dad. 'You'll ruin the upholstery.'
'You're not getting into the car like that,'
said Mum. 'You'll catch your death of cold.
Get those wet things off.'
I took off my squelchy shoes.
I took off my soggy socks.
And stopped.
'And the rest,' said Mum.
'No, Mum, please.'
'No one will see.'
'I can see,' said my brother.

'No looking.'
Off came the saturated shorts.
'I can see his pants.
I can see his pants.
And they're wet,' said my brother helpfully.

'They're not.'
'Get them off,' said Mum.
'No, Mum, please.'
'Don't be such a big drip.
Are you going to take them off
Or shall I?'
Down came the pants.
I sat on a towel in the car
next to my brother who was near wetting himself with
   laughter.
'What's it like to
What's it like to
What's it like to
have no pants?'

'Mum. Tell him.
Mum?
Dad?
Stop laughing.
It's not funny.'
'You're right,' said Dad.
There was a moment's silence
Then they all started laughing again.
Could my life ever reach a lower ebb?
It did at the end of our road.

'Oh. Isn't that Pamela Whitethorn?'
said my brother.
'Where?'
I looked.
It was.
'You love her.'
'I don't.'
'Do. Otherwise you wouldn't be blushing.'
'I'm not blushing.
People always go red when they've fallen in the river
Everybody knows that.'
'Shall I tell her you haven't got any pants on?'
'You dare.'
'That's enough,' said Mum.

The shame.
Pantless before Pamela.

Through the window, I peeped at Pamela.
She was looking right at me.
Pamela knew things.
She knew where babies came from.
I wondered whether boys sitting in cars with no pants on
Looked any different to boys sitting in cars with pants on.
I waved in a casual 'I've got my pants on' sort of way.
If there was a difference
Pamela would know.

John Coldwell

24

Comical Folk

In a cottage in Fife
Lived a man and his wife
Who, believe me, were comical folk;
For, to people's surprise,
They both saw with their eyes,
And their tongues moved whenever they spoke!

When they were asleep,
I'm told, that to keep
Their eyes open they could not contrive;
They both walked on their feet,
And 'twas thought what they eat
Helped, with drinking, to keep them alive!

Anon.

25

Jabbermockery

'Twas Thursday and the bottom set
Did gyre and gimble in the gym.
All mimsy was Miss Borogrove
And the Head of Maths was grim.

'Beware the Mathematix, my friend!
His sums that snarl. His co-ordinates that catch!
Beware the Deputy Bird, and shun
The evil Earring-snatch!'

She took her ballpoint pen in hand:
Long time the problem's end she sought –
So rested she by the lavatory
And sat awhile in thought.

And as in toughish thought she sat,
The Mathematix with eyes of flame
Came calculating through the cloakroom doors
And subtracted as he came.

She thought real fast as he went past;
The well placed soap went slickersmack!
She left him stunned and with the sums
She went galumphing back.

'And hast thou got the answers, Jackie?
Come to our desk,' beamed idle boys.
'Oh, frabjous day, Quelle heure! Calais!'
They chortled in their joy.

'Twas Thursday and the bottom set
Did gyre and gimble in the gym.
All mimsy was Miss Borogrove
And the Head of Maths was **grim**.

Trevor Millum

Peter Piper

Peter Piper picked a peck of pickled peppers;
A peck of pickled peppers Peter Piper picked.
If Peter Piper picked a peck of pickled peppers,
Where's the peck of pickled peppers Peter Piper picked?

Anon.

Bus Queue

Seventeen people
Waiting ages for a bus
Then two came at once

Paul Cookson

Down in Witches Dell

Absconded from primary school
and another day of swirling torment
beside my childhood dream girl;
in the pond within the wood
a stick stood
strangely upright.
I dreamed it was Excalibur,
waded in and fished it out
splashed back to the bank
made out our initials
on the blank bark,
then waving the wand about
I wished a bond between us
a fondness that wouldn't fade
a sticking together for tomorrow
and for ever
in the spreading future
beyond the deadly nightshade.
Meanwhile in the playground she was snogging someone else.

John Hegley

29

Up in Smoke

Cornelius loved Chemistry
It had a strange attraction
The final words he spoke were 'Sir,
Is this a chain reaction?'

Paul Bright

30

The Hippopotamus Song

A bold Hippopotamus was standing one day
On the banks of the cool Shalimar.
He gazed at the bottom as it peacefully lay
By the light of the evening star.
Away on a hilltop sat combing her hair
His fair Hippopotamine maid;
The Hippopotamus was no ignoramus
And sang her this sweet serenade.

Mud, Mud, glorious mud,
Nothing quite like it for cooling the blood!
So follow me, follow
Down to the hollow
And there let us wallow
In glorious mud!

The fair Hippopotama he aimed to entice
From her seat on that hilltop above,
As she hadn't got a ma to give her advice,
Came tiptoeing down to her love.
Like thunder the forest re-echoed the sound
Of the song that they sang as they met.
His inamorata adjusted her garter
And lifted her voice in duet.

Mud, Mud, glorious mud,
Nothing quite like it for cooling the blood!
So follow me, follow,
Down to the hollow
And there let us wallow
In glorious mud!

Now more Hippopotami began to convene
On the banks of that river so wide.
I wonder now what am I to say of the scene
That ensued by the Shalimar side?
They dived all at once with an ear-splitting splosh
Then rose to the surface again,
A regular army of Hippopotami
All singing this haunting refrain.

Mud! Mud! Glorious mud!
Nothing quite like it for cooling the blood.
So follow me, follow,
Down to the hollow
And there let us wallow
In glorious mud!

Michael Flanders

My Cousin Melda

My Cousin Melda
she don't make fun
she ain't afraid of anyone
even mosquitoes
when they bite her
she does bite them back
and say –
'Now tell me, how you like that?'

Grace Nichols

June

Wiwis

To amuse
emus
on warm summer nights

Kiwis
do wiwis
from spectacular heights.

Roger McGough

Starter

Hi!
I'm Cousin Art
And I like to start
A new thing every day.
But I never finish anything
At least that's what . . .
they . . .

Tony Bradman

3

Betty Botter

Betty Botter bought some butter,
But, she said, this butter's bitter;
If I put it in my batter,
It will make my batter bitter,
But a bit of better butter
Will make my batter better.
So she bought a bit of butter
Better than her bitter butter,
And she put it in her batter,
And it made her batter better,
So 'twas better Betty Botter
Bought a bit of better butter.

Anon.

How to Successfully Persuade Your Parents to Give You More Pocket Money

Ask, request, demand, suggest, cajole or charm
Ingratiate, suck up to, flatter, compliment or smarm
Negotiate, debate, discuss, persuade, convince, explain
Or reason, justify, protest, object, dispute, complain
Propose, entreat, beseech, beg, plead, appeal, implore
Harass, go on about it, pester, whinge, whine, nag and bore
Annoy, insult, reproach, denounce, squeal, scream and
   shout
Go quiet, subdued, look worried, fret, brood, tremble,
   shiver, pout
Act depressed, downhearted, upset, snivel, sigh
Go all glum and plaintive, wobble bottom lip and cry
Sniff, sulk, grumble, stare at ceiling, mope, pine, stay in bed
Get cross, get angry, fume, seethe, fester, agitate, see red
Provoke, enrage, push, bully, aggravate and goad
Screech, smoke, burn up, ignite, spark, detonate, EXPLODE

And if all that doesn't work

Here are two little tricks
That should do it with ease

No 1: smile
No 2: say please.

Andrea Shavick

The Invisible Man's Invisible Dog

My invisible dog is not much fun.
I don't know if he's sad or glum.
I don't know if, when I pat his head,
I'm really patting his bum instead.

Brian Patten

The Purple Cow

I never saw a Purple Cow,
I never hope to see one;
But I can tell you, anyhow,
I'd rather see than be one.

Gelett Burgess

7

Garden Shed

A
garden
shed, a garden
shed, my head is like
a garden shed: it's full of junk and
flower pots, wellie boots and who knows what.

No, really though, my head is crammed
you can't get in, the door is jammed:
with things I've seen, things I've said
things I've done and things I've read.
Plus everything I've thought about
. . . if I was you – I'd just keep out!!

James Carter

Twinkle, twinkle, little bat

Twinkle, twinkle, little bat!
How I wonder what you're at!
Up above the world you fly,
Like a tea-tray in the sky.

Lewis Carroll

Where's Grandma?

Ever since my little brother
Buried Grandad on the beach,
We've have to keep Grandma
Out of reach.

We hid her in the attic
But he very nearly had her
When he poked her with his spade
After climbing up the ladder.

Ever since my little brother
Buried Grandad in the sand,
Grandma's been complaining he's
Out of hand.

It's just a phase, my mother said,
My brother will soon chuck it,
But the last we saw of Grandma
Was my brother's empty bucket . . .

Celia Warren

10

A Tale of Two Citizens

I have a Russian friend who lives in Minsk
And wears a lofty hat of beaver skinsk
(Which does not suit a man so tall and thinsk).
He has a frizzly beard upon his chinsk.
He keeps his britches up with safety pinsk.
  'They're so much better than those thingsk
  Called belts and brackies, don't you thinksk?'
  You'll hear him say, the man from Minsk.

He has a Polish pal who's from Gdansk,
Who lives by selling drinksk to football fansk,
And cheese rolls, from a little caravansk.
(He finds it pleasanter than robbing banksk.)
He also uses pinsk to hold his pantsk.
  'Keep up one's pantsk with rubber bandsk!?
  It can't be donesk! It simply can'tsk!
  Not in Gdansk!' he'll say. 'No thanksk!'

They're so alikesk that strangers often thinksk
That they are brothers, yesk, or even twinsk.
'I live in Minsk but I was born in Omsk,'
Says one. His friend replies, 'That's where *I'm* fromsk!
Perhaps we're brothers after all, not friendsk.'
    So they wrote homesk and asked their mumsk
    But found they weren'tsk; so they shook handsk
    And left for Minsk, and for Gdansk.

Gerard Benson

Last

We see The Straggler as often as it rains

                                    – skinny
hairless legs, a wheezing chest, dilapidated pumps
and blue cross-country kit –

                           stopping for directions
at the supermarkets built since he began

'Who changed the roads?'

                           'Who moved the park?'
'I could have sworn

              this was the way'

                       Perplexed
he staggers off

              through drifts of leaves or snow
forbidden to catch a bus

                   or – if he knew of any –
follow short cuts back to school

                      Weeds breaking
through the playground

                 crack by crack

                     the names

on every desk long gone
                    his blazer alone
hangs from a peg
               in the draughty changing room

Stephen Knight

Dad, the Amateur Hypnotist

Follow
               my
swinging
               watch
with
               your
eyes.
               Now
you
               are
feeling
               sleepy . . .
When
               I

count
to
three
and
click
my
fingers,
you
will
wake
up,
then
bark
like
a
dog.
One.
Two.
Three.
        Click!
        'Miaow.'

Mike Johnson

Bengal

There once was a man of Bengal
Who was asked to a fancy dress ball;
　　He murmured: 'I'll risk it
　　and go as a biscuit . . .'
But a dog ate him up in the hall.

Anon.

14

Second Look at the Proverbs

People who live in glass houses
Should watch it while changing their trouziz.

Gerard Benson

What a Wonderful Bird

What a wonderful bird the frog are –
When he sit, he stand almost;
When he hop, he fly almost.
He ain't got no sense hardly;
He ain't got no tail hardly either.
When he sit, he sit on what it ain't got – almost.

Anon.

Heather Potts

Heather Potts is awfully thin.
She's lighter than a feather,
Which makes her interesting to watch
In very windy weather.

Cynthia Rider

194

17

Where's that Gorilla?

'I had it with me just a moment ago,' said Mum.
'Do me a favour?
Nip upstairs and bring me down the Gorilla.'
'A Gorilla?
Upstairs?
What?
In our house?'
'Yes, you heard,' said Mum.
'And don't be bringing me down some marmoset
And saying,
"Will this do instead?"'
'Can't Tom go?'
'He's busy with the Giraffe
And besides,
I'm asking you.'

Up the stairs
Tip toeing over terrapins
Now where would she have put the gorilla?
Check the bathroom first
Full of penguins.
'Seen the Gorilla?'
Splash! No.
Try the toilet.
Full of hippo.
'Seen the Gorilla?'
'No. And shut the door. I haven't finished in here yet.'
Search Mum and Dad's bedroom.
Boa Constrictor, Ant Eater
'Seen the gorilla?'
'Try the bathroom.'
'Just did.'
'Your bedroom?'
Not a chance.

I tidied it yesterday
Swept up the frogs,
Hung up the bats in size order
And emptied the elephant
But I ask all the same,
'Seen the gorilla?'
'Try the toilet.'
'I told you, I'm busy.'
Tom's room?
He's wedged a hedgehog under the door
I can't get in.

Back down the stairs
Toe tipping over terrapins

'I can't find the gorilla or anything like one.'
'You'll never believe this,' said Mum
'I had it with me all the time
Under the cushions.'
And there it was –
The great hairy thing.
'Oh **that** Gorilla.'
'What do you mean?' asked Mum.
'How many gorillas did you think we had?'

John Coldwell

Cry for Help

To whoever finds this note.

Me and twenty-three others
are trapped in a large pie
at King's.
Take this to Special Branch
and earn yourself a
nest egg reward.

Blackbird.

John C. Desmond

19

The Day I Got My Finger Stuck
up My Nose

When I got my finger stuck up my nose
I went to a doctor, who said,
'Nothing like this has happened before,
We will have to chop off your head.'

'It's only my finger stuck up my nose,
It's only my finger!' I said.
'I can see what it is,' the doctor replied,
'But we'll have to chop off your head.'

He went to the cabinet. He took out an axe.
I watched with considerable dread.
'But it's only my finger stuck up my nose.
It's only a finger!' I said.

'Perhaps we can yank it out with a hook
Tied to some surgical thread.
Maybe we can try that,' he replied,
'Rather than chop off your head.'

'I'm never going to pick it again.
I've now learned my lesson,' I said.
'I won't stick my finger up my nose –
I'll stick it in my ear instead.'

Brian Patten

Answer Phone

Please leave your name.
I shall call you back.
There is no one here.
Do you have a number?

Do you have a cat?
I have four children.
They keep me busy.
They should be back.

I shall call your number.
My mind is empty.
There is no one there.
Please leave my name.

Please leave my cat.
He has no number.
Do you want four children?
They have names.

Please name your children.
My cat is Rover.
He will call you back.
I keep him busy.

John Mole

21

Magic Cat

My mum whilst walking through the door
Spilt some magic on the floor.
Blobs of this
and splots of that
but most of it upon the cat.

Our cat turned magic, straight away
and in the garden went to play
where it grew two massive wings
and flew around in fancy rings.
'Oh look!' cried Mother, pointing high,
'I didn't know our cat could fly.'
Then with a dash of Tibby's tail
she turned my mum into a snail!

So now she lives beneath a stone
and dusts around a different home.
And I'm an ant
and Dad's a mouse
And Tibby's living in our house.

Peter Dixon

22

I sat next to the duchess at tea

I sat next to the duchess at tea
It was just as I feared it would be.
Her rumblings abdominal
Were simply phenomenal
And everyone thought it was me!

Anon.

A Good Poem

I like a good poem,
one with lots of fighting
in it. Blood, and the
clanging of armour. Poems

against Scotland are good,
and poems that defeat
the French with crossbows.
I don't like poems that

aren't about anything.
Sonnets are wet and
a waste of time.
Also poems that don't

know how to rhyme.
If I was a poem
I'd play football and
get picked for England.

Roger McGough

Knickers

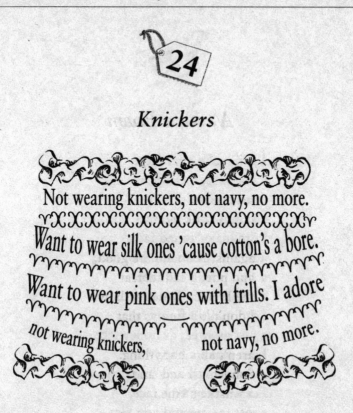

Not wearing knickers, not navy, no more.

Want to wear silk ones 'cause cotton's a bore.

Want to wear pink ones with frills. I adore

not wearing knickers, not navy, no more.

Gina Douthwaite

Make a Face

I can make a fat face,
a dog face, a cat face.
I can make a thin face,
a skinny little pin face.
I can make a mad face,
a horrid, mean and bad face,
a sick face, a sad face,
a rather like my dad face.
I can make a funny face,
a just as sweet as honey face.
I can make a happy face,
a sharp snarl and snappy face.
I can make a true face,
a just for me and you face.
But this face,
you ain't seen this face –
NO PLACE!

Tony Mitton

26

On Top of Spaghetti

On top of spaghetti, all covered with cheese,
I lost my poor meatball when somebody sneezed.

It rolled off the table, and on to the floor,
And then my poor meatball rolled out of the door.

It rolled into the garden, and under a bush,
And then my poor meatball was nothing but mush.

The mush was as tasty, as tasty can be,
And early next summer, it grew into a tree.

The tree was all covered, with beautiful moss,
It grew lovely meatballs and tomato sauce.

So if you eat spaghetti, all covered with cheese,
Hold on to your meatball, and don't ever sneeze.

Anon.

Superheroes I Could Have Been

After accidentally rescuing planet Earth
I was offered the chance
To become a superhero.
Unfortunately all the best positions
Had gone.
This is what was left:

Liquid Refreshment Machine Repairman
(A lifesaver on a hot day)
Mosquito Man
(Keeps insects at bay)
Salting Icy Roads Man
(Saving skidding lorries and cars)
Confectionery Dispenser Unit Man
(Saving melting chocolate bars)
Tadpole man
(Rescuing frogs from logs)
Stick Insect Man
(rescuing stick insects from frogs)
Ten Pence Down the Back of the Sofa Man
(Where only the bravest superheroes go)
And, of course, Supergran
(but I don't somehow think so)

I could have been Captain Decisive
But I couldn't make up my mind
I could have been Captain King of the Hill
But I didn't feel so inclined
I could have been Captain Upholsterer
But I'd never have recovered
I could have been Captain Apathy
But I couldn't be bothered

Roger Stevens

28

For Brownie (the Goldfish)

For Brownie
(the goldfish)
This Christmas
I bought
A friend to play with
But since Mr Piranha arrived
I have not seen Brownie
I expect they are playing
Hide and Seek.

Peter Dixon

29

Here's What They Are

A Meter Bay –
A Parking Space.

A Teacher's Desk –
A Marking Place.

The Park, for Dogs –
A Barking Space.

The Deep Blue Sea –
A Sharking Place.

Mount Ararat –
An Arking Space.

The Slides and Swings –
A Larking Place.

And deep Black Holes –
A 'Dark' in Space!

Trevor Harvey

30

E-PET-APH

Gerbil Gerry made a mess
When he got trapped in the trouser press.
It's sad to say, the truth is that
Both of us now feel quite flat.
Poor old pet with a permanent crease,
Gerry Gerbil, *Pressed In Peace.*

Andrew Fusek Peters

July

King Arthur's Knights

King Arthur's knights were chivalrous
When sat around his table,
But even they were frivolous
Whenever they were able,
And in the moat at Camelot
They splashed about and swam a lot.

Colin West

Playing Tennis with Justin

It's dinnertime and very sunny
I'm on the yard playing tennis with Justin.
Justin is winning fifty-five nil.

He's got a proper tennis bat called a rocket
I haven't got one so he gave me his spare one.
His rocket is filled up with string, mine isn't
Mine's got lots of holes.

If I hit the ball with the bit with no holes
It goes quite a long way, but usually
Justin says I've hit the net.

We haven't got a net but Justin says
He knows where it would be
If we did have one.
Justin's very clever like that.

He's just scored fifteen more points
I nearly scored one a moment ago
But Justin said it was offside.
So the score is seventy-nil to him.

Justin says that my score is called love
Not nil, well I don't love it much
I keep losing, Justin says not to worry
I might score a six in a minute.

He says it's his second serve for juice
Well, the dinner lady hasn't called our group
In yet, so I haven't had one serving or any juice
I'm starving and it's very hot.

Justin says he's scored three more goals
And I should keep my eye on the ball
Then I might hit it with my rocket.

If Justin doesn't shut up quick
I might hit him with my rocket
I think tennis is rubbish.

Justin says we can play at cricket
But I've got to go in goals
Sometimes you just can't win.

David Harmer

3

If You Should Meet a Crocodile

If you should meet a crocodile,
  Don't take a stick and poke him;
Ignore the welcome in his smile,
  Be careful not to stroke him.
For he sleeps upon the Nile,
  He thinner gets and thinner;
But whene'er you meet a crocodile
  He's ready for his dinner.

Anon.

4

Ark Anglers

Noah let his sons go fishing
Only on the strictest terms:
'Sit still, keep quiet and concentrate,
We've only got two worms!'

Celia Warren

Lettuce Marry

Do you carrot all for me?
My heart beets for you,
With your turnip nose
And your radish face.
You are a peach.
If we cantaloupe
Lettuce marry;
Weed make a swell pear.

Anon.

When I Was Young

I had two pairs of shoes
(One for everyday and one for best)
The best ones only came out on Sundays
I would have to stuff my feet into them
Curl them up like fists 'til they burnt and hurt so much
That I'd end up walking to church on my hands

When I was young . . .
Vegetables were a luxury
Carrots were not all the same size
They were knobbly, covered in dirt
And resembled wizened old people
You didn't much like

When I was young . . .
You could have bread and butter
Or bread and jam – never both
Tangerines only appeared at Christmas
At the bottom of a very sweaty sock
With toenails in it

When I was young . . .
We played out in the street
Until we had so many scabs on our knees
That we'd have to go indoors
And pick them off while we listened to the wireless

My idea of luxury
Was a pickled egg

My idea of heaven
Was a scratchy jersey
which had such tight sleeves
That your hands would turn blue
And threaten to drop off

Our idea of fun
Was to laugh at each other's jumpers
and take bets on whose hands
Would drop off first.

Lindsay MacRae

7

The Leader

I wanna be the leader
I wanna be the leader
Can I be the leader?
Can I? I can?
Promise? Promise?
Yippee, I'm the leader
I'm the leader

OK what shall we do?

Roger McGough

Short Visit, Long Stay

The school trip was a special occasion
But we never reached our destination
Instead of the Zoo
I was locked in the loo
Of an M62 Service Station.

Paul Cookson

The Greatest of Them All

You can keep your superheroes
Like Batman and the rest –
My dad can beat 'em all hands down,
He really is the best.

He tears up toilet tissues,
He can break a twig in two,
He can lift a bag of feathers,
No, there's nothing he can't do.

He can bend a piece of cardboard,
He can frighten new-born flies,
And at snapping off a daisy head
He always takes first prize.

He's stronger than a sparrow
And he's faster than a snail,
He can punch a hole in newspapers
And never ever fail.

He's thinner than a matchstick
And his biceps look like peas,
His legs are like a spider's
And he's got two knobbly knees.

He's a legend in his lifetime
He's a hero through and through.
And what's the name we know him by?
It's *Superwimp* – that's who!

Clive Webster

My Man, Jeffrey
(after 'Jubilate Agno' by Christopher Smart)

For I consider him my man, Jeffrey.

For he is warm as a blanket to sit on.

For he's a wiz with a tin opener and with a spoon.

For he ignores it whenever I sharpen my claws on the legs of even his favourite chair.

For he's provided the curtains I shred for my bedding and says they were old anyway.

For he is funny when he plays with my toys – while I watch.

For he loves The Premiership which looks very like men chasing one big fat mouse.

For he loves flattening my fur till I purr

For then I fall fast asleep in his lap.

For he brings puddles of milk I can lap.

For he throws cans when he's in a bad temper.

For he forgives me before I forgive him.

For he's an ape from the jungle at heart.

For he knows I am a lion, and therefore his master.

Jill Townsend

The Fly

God in his wisdom made the fly
And then forgot to tell us why.

Ogden Nash

House Party

The houses had a party
they invited all their friends –
the semis and the terraced
the middles and the ends.
    They invited all the chalets,
    high-rise blocks of flats,
    caravans and castles,
    homes for dogs and cats.

They invited all the bungalows,
houses from Peru,
scrapers from Big Apple,
huts from Timbuktu.
The igloos came,
the teepees,
pagodas and a cave,
an ant hill,
and a beehive,
a police house
and a nave.

It was a lovely party –
the church house did some chants,
the summer house brought sunshine,
and the greenhouse brought the plants.
   The lighthouse winked a message
   for peace within each house . . .
   'Hallelujah' sang the angels
   'Hallelujah' sighed the mouse.

Peter Dixon

There Was an Old Man with a Beard

There was an Old Man with a beard,
Who said, 'It is just as I feared! –
  Two Owls and a Hen,
  Four Larks and a Wren,
Have all built their nests in my beard!'

Edward Lear

14

When the Aliens Came to Dinner

When the aliens came to dinner
Their manners were a delight,

Well . . .

It's true that they nibbled the napkins,
It's true that they had a small fight,
It's true that they waggled their eyeballs,
It's true that they bent all the spoons,
It's true that they wore our best lampshades,
And swung round the room like baboons,
It's true that they ate with their feelers,
Instead of their forks and their knives,
It's true that they flicked their spaghetti
At some rather smart men (plus their wives),
It's true that they jumped in the jelly,
It's true that they stole a whole pie,

But . . .

They thanked us all EVER SO nicely
When the time came to wave us Good Bye.

Clare Bevan

15

The Uncomfortable Truth

Robin Hood
Was very good
At dropping down from trees
To take by force
Both man and horse
With fabled expertise

But truth admits
The awkward bits
Like when he overshot 'em –
Robin Hood
Was also good
At landing on his bottom.

John Mole

16

Puffer Fish

Those who think this little fish'll

Make a very tasty dish'll

Find as dinner starts to bristle

That they've bitten on a thistle!

Liz Brownlee

17

Borrowed Time

Great-Gran is ninety-six.
'I'm living on borrowed time,'
she said.

'Who did you borrow it from?'
asked my little sister.

'Never you mind,' said Gran.

'I hope you said thank you,'
said my sister.

Great-Gran laughed.
'I do,' she said.
'Every single day.'

John Foster

Where Do All the Teachers Go?

Where do all the teachers go
When it's four o'clock?
Do they live in houses
And do they wash their socks?

Do they wear pyjamas
And do they watch TV?
And do they pick their noses
The same as you and me?

Do they live with other people
Have they mums and dads?
And were they ever children
And were they ever bad?

Did they ever, never spell right
Did they ever make mistakes?
Were they punished in the corner
If they pinched the chocolate flakes?

Did they ever lose their hymn books
Did they ever leave their greens?
Did they scribble on the desk tops
Did they wear old dirty jeans?

I'll follow one back home today
I'll find out what they do
Then I'll put it in a poem
That they can read to you.

Peter Dixon

All the Trappings

Said The Mummy, 'I'm starting to find
That this job is a bit of a bind.
   Though I'm white as a sheet
   And feel dead on my feet
I just don't get the chance to *unwind*!'

Graham Denton

20

There Was an Old Lady

There was an old lady who swallowed a fly.
I don't know why she swallowed a fly.
Perhaps she'll die.

Poor old lady, she swallowed a spider.
It squirmed and wriggled and turned inside her.
She swallowed the spider to catch the fly.
I don't know why she swallowed a fly.
Perhaps she'll die.

Poor old lady, she swallowed a bird.
How absurd! She swallowed a bird.
She swallowed the bird to catch the spider,
She swallowed the spider to catch the fly.
I don't know why she swallowed a fly.
Perhaps she'll die.

Poor old lady, she swallowed a cat.
Think of that! She swallowed a cat.
She swallowed the cat to catch the bird.
She swallowed the bird to catch the spider,
She swallowed the spider to catch the fly.
I don't know why she swallowed a fly.
Perhaps she'll die.

Poor old lady, she swallowed a dog.
She went the whole hog when she swallowed the dog.
She swallowed the dog to catch the cat,
She swallowed the cat to catch the bird.
She swallowed the bird to catch the spider,
She swallowed the spider to catch the fly,
I don't know why she swallowed a fly.
Perhaps she'll die.

Poor old lady, she swallowed a cow.
I don't know how she swallowed the cow.
She swallowed the cow to catch the dog,
She swallowed the dog to catch the cat,
She swallowed the cat to catch the bird.
She swallowed the bird to catch the spider,
She swallowed the spider to catch the fly.
I don't know why she swallowed a fly.
Perhaps she'll die.

Poor old lady, she swallowed a horse.
She died, of course.

Anon.

The Magician's Garden

Pluck a peonie in the magician's garden
and in your hand
it turns into a fluttering white dove.

From out of the large upturned flowerpot
a white rabbit hops,
and on the far side of the lawn
Dolores, the gardener's lovely assistant
dressed in a spangly swimsuit,
disappears into the potting shed.

Shazam! She reappears
from behind the compost heap
on the far side of the garden

The privet hedges gaze
in silent astonishment as
yard after yard of brilliantly coloured
chiffon scarves
gushes from the watering can.
'Bravo!' cries the crow. 'Bravo!'

Mick Gowar

The Clown's Garden

In the clown's garden the blackbirds blare out
Tea for Two cha-cha-cha! –
honking out the chorus
like a quartet of raucous clarinets,
while the sparrows cat call
and blow raspberries from the raspberry bushes.

The rake lies prongs up
in the long grass, ready to catapult up
and smack an unsuspecting patsy
in the face, while the hose runs amok,
soaking the red-nosed gardener.

Don't bend down to smell the flowers
unless you want a jet
of jet black ink
all down the front
of your clean white shirt.

But don't flinch when the gardener's boy
comes running with a heavy watering can
and trips . . .
it's only full of silver paper stars.

And at the day's end, the grand finale:
with an enormous bang
the handles come off the lawnmower,
the grassbox turns upside down
and the wheels fall off.

Mick Gowar

On Nevski Bridge

On Nevski Bridge a Russian stood
Chewing his beard for lack of food.
Said he, 'It's tough this stuff to eat
But a darn sight better than shredded wheat!'

Anon.

Property for Sale

Two houses up for sale.
One stick, one straw.
Both self-assembly.
See pig next door.

Rachel Rooney

Sky in the Pie!

Waiter, there's a sky in my pie
Remove it at once if you please
You can keep your incredible sunsets
I ordered mincemeat and cheese

I can't stand nightingales singing
Or clouds all burnished with gold
The whispering breeze is disturbing the peas
And making my chips go all cold

I don't care if the chef is an artist
Whose canvases hang in the Tate
I want two veg. and puff pastry
Not the Universe heaped on my plate

OK I'll try just a spoonful
I suppose I've got nothing to lose
Mm . . . the colours quite tickle the palette
With a blend of delicate hues

The sun has a custardy flavour
And the clouds are as light as air
And the wind a chewier texture
(With a hint of cinnamon there?)

This sky is simply delicious
Why haven't I tried it before?
I can chew my way through to Eternity
And still have room left for more.

Having acquired a taste for the Cosmos
I'll polish this sunset off soon
I can't wait to tuck into the night sky
Waiter! Please bring me the Moon!

Roger McGough

26

(You Ain't Nothing But A) Hedgehog

You ain't nothing but a hedgehog
Foragin' all the time
You ain't nothing but a hedgehog
Foragin' all the time
You ain't never pricked a predator
You ain't no porcupine.

John Cooper Clarke

27

Clichés

Every cloud has a silver lining;
Every rainbow, its pot of gold;
Every parting is such sweet sorrow;
Every story's a tale to be told;
Every joy is a joy for sharing;
Every bridge is just meant to be crossed;

Every day brings a new tomorrow;
Every win means that someone has lost;
Every song is a song worth singing;
Every dream has a chance to come true;
Every friend is a friend worth knowing –
So why am I lumbered with you?

Trevor Harvey

Tomato Ketchup

If you do not shake the bottle,
None'll come and then a lot'll . . .

Anon.

29

Some Sayings that Never Caught On

He's as daft as a pineapple!
Time is just like custard!
She swims like a cactus!

He's as daft as a cactus!
Time is just like a pineapple!
She swims like custard!

He's as daft as custard!
Time is just like a cactus!
She swims like a pineapple!

Ian McMillan

Monster Sale!!

'MONSTER SALE!!' the advert said.
I'm telling you – it LIED.
There was junk galore
In the Super Store . . .
But not ONE monster inside.

Clare Bevan

31

Grandma Was Eaten by a Shark!

Grandma was eaten by a shark
Dad, by a killer whale
And my baby brother got slurped up
By a rather hungry sea snail.

A cuttlefish cut my mum to bits
An octopus strangled my sister
A jellyfish stung my auntie's toes
Giving her terrible blisters.

A pufferfish poisoned my grandpa
A dogfish ate my cat
And then a catfish ate my dog!
I was very upset about that.

So you go for a swim if you like
Just don't ask me to come too
I'm staying here with my camera
I can't wait to see what gets you!

Andrea Shavick

August

Ryde

There was a young lady of Ryde
Who ate a green apple and died;
  The apple fermented
  Inside the lamented,
And made cider inside her inside.

Anon.

The Cow

The cow is of the bovine ilk;
One end is moo, the other, milk.

Ogden Nash

Colonel Fazackerley

Colonel Fazackerley Butterworth-Toast
Bought an old castle complete with a ghost,
But someone or other forgot to declare
To Colonel Fazack that the spectre was there.

On the very first evening, while waiting to dine,
The Colonel was taking a fine sherry wine,
When the ghost, with a furious flash and a flare,
Shot out of the chimney and shivered, 'Beware!'

Colonel Fazackerley put down his glass
And said, 'My dear fellow, that's really first class!
I just can't conceive how you do it at all.
I imagine you're going to a Fancy Dress Ball?'

At this, the dread ghost gave a withering cry.
Said the Colonel (his monocle firm in his eye),
'Now just how you do it I wish I could think.
Do sit down and tell me, and please have a drink.'

The ghost in his phosphorous cloak gave a roar
And floated about between ceiling and floor.
He walked through a wall and returned through a pane
And backed up the chimney and came down again.

Said the Colonel, 'With laughter I'm feeling quite weak!'
(As trickles of merriment ran down his cheek).
'My house-warming party I hope you won't spurn.
You *must* say you'll come and you'll give us a turn!'

Whereupon, the poor spectre – quite out of his wits –
Proceeded to shake himself almost to bits.
He rattled his chains and he clattered his bones
And he filled the whole castle with mumbles and moans.

But Colonel Fazackerley, just as before,
Was simply delighted and called out, 'Encore!'
At which the ghost vanished, his efforts in vain,
And never was seen at the castle again.

'Oh dear, what a pity!' said Colonel Fazack.
'I don't know his name, so I can't call him back.'
And then with a smile that was hard to define,
Colonel Fazackerley went in to dine.

Charles Causley

4

Letter to a Dead Dog

Dear Dirk,
I'm sorry you're dead.
Not as sorry as old Mrs Jones next door
but then, you were hers.
Still, we did have some good times together
didn't we, Dirk?
You digging a hole under the hedge, me filling it in . . .
you digging a hole under the hedge, me filling it in . . .
that was, until you discovered
how to get up on to the compost bin
and jump over the wall.
And I don't blame you, not at all,
for the eleven assorted balls
you managed to maul, puncture,
cover with slobber,
tear to shreds.
Pugs will be pugs.

And towards the end we were real mates.
Remember, Dirk, all those walks
to the park and the shops? (That was after
you'd wrapped your lead round Mrs Jones
trying to kill Askey's milk float
and left her with both legs in plaster).
Remember the Alsatian,
the one you bit on the nose?
I saved you, Dirk, no doubt about it.
Had the trainers, jeans
and an ear bashing from Mum to prove it.
Did I complain when you hid in my sports bag
and infested my shorts with fleas
or sneaked upstairs and tried to lick
Gruesome Galactic Monsters
from my computer screen?

Mum says you had a peaceful end
lying outside our back kitchen door
with a half-eaten T-bone steak
gripped in your jaws.
So I reckon, wherever you are,
you must be in a good mood which
I hope you are because
there's a favour I need to ask.
You know that last thing of mine you stole –
grey, twelve centimetres long, made those quirky noises
if you managed to get your teeth in the right spot?
PLEASE could you, your ghost or *something* get in touch
and tell me WHERE YOU BURIED IT!
I know you thought it was some kinky hi-tech bone
but it wasn't.
It was my mobile phone.

Patricia Leighton

Crazy Days

'Twas midnight on the ocean,
Not a streetcar was in sight;
The sun was shining brightly,
For it rained all day that night.

'Twas a summer day in winter
And snow was raining fast,
As a barefoot boy with shoes on
Stood sitting in the grass.

Anon.

6

Stickleback

The Stickleback's a spiky chap,
  Worse than a bit of briar.
Hungry Pike would sooner swallow
  Embers from a fire.

The Stickleback is fearless in
  The way he loves his wife.
Every minute of the day
  He guards her with his life.

She, like him, is dressed to kill
  In stiff and steely prickles,
And when they kiss, there bubbles up
  The laughter of the tickles.

Ted Hughes

The Duck

Behold the duck.
It does not cluck.
A cluck it lacks.
It quacks.
It is specially fond
Of a puddle or pond.
When it dines or sups,
It bottoms ups.

Ogden Nash

8

The Prime Minister Is Ten Today

This morning I abolished
homework, detention and dinner ladies.
I outlawed lumpy custard, school mashed spuds
and handwriting lessons.
From now on play-times must last two hours
unless it rains, in which case we all go home
except the teachers who must do extra PE
outside in the downpour.

Whispering behind your hand in class
must happen each morning between ten and twelve,
and each child needs only do
ten minutes' work in one school hour.

I've passed a No Grumpy Teacher law
so one bad word or dismal frown
from Mr Spite or Miss Hatchetface
will get them each a month's stretch
sharpening pencils and marking books
inside the gaol of their choice.

All headteachers are forbidden
from wearing soft-soled shoes
instead they must wear wooden clogs
so you can hear them coming.
They are also banned from shouting
or spoiling our assembly by pointing
at the ones who never listen.

Finally the schools must shut
for at least half the year
and if the weather's really sunny
the teachers have to take us all
to the seaside for the day.

If you've got some good ideas
for other laws about the grown-ups
drop me a line in Downing Street
I'll always be glad to listen
come on, help me change a thing or two
before we all grow up
and get boring.

David Harmer

Song Sung by a Man on a Barge to Another Man on a Different Barge in Order to Drive Him Mad

Oh,

I am the best bargee bar none,
You are the best bargee bar one!
You are the second-best bargee,
You are the best bargee bar me!

Oh,

I am the best . . .

(and so on, until he is
hurled into the canal)

Kit Wright

10

Mafia Cats

We're the Mafia cats
  Bugsy, Franco and Toni
We're crazy for pizza
  With hot pepperoni

We run all the rackets
  From gambling to vice
On St Valentine's Day
  We massacre mice

We always wear shades
  To show that we're meanies
Big hats and sharp suits
  And drive Lamborghinis

We're the Mafia cats
  Bugsy, Franco and Toni
Love Sicilian wine
  And cheese macaroni

But we have a secret
  (And if you dare tell
You'll end up with the kitten
  At the bottom of the well

Or covered in concrete
  And thrown into the deep
For this is one secret
  You really must keep).

We're the Cosa Nostra
  Run the scams and the fiddles
But at home we are
  Mopsy, Ginger and Tiddles.

(Breathe one word and you're cat-meat. OK?)

Roger McGough

Neversaurus

When dinosaurs roamed the earth,
So huge, it was easy to spot 'em,
You'd frequently see a triceratops,
But never a tricerabottom.

Celia Warren

Somewhere!

Somewhere in the halls of wisdom
Lies the largest box.
Filled with all life's little mysteries
And my missing socks!

Ian Deal

262

13

Although

Although
I had

butterflies
in my
stomach

and ants
in my pants

and a bee
in my
bonnet

and a flea
in my
ear –

I had
a whale
of a time.

Tony Langham

14

My Mum's Put Me on the Transfer List

On Offer:
one nippy striker, ten years old
has scored seven goals this season
has nifty footwork and a big smile
knows how to dive in the penalty box
can get filthy and muddy within two minutes
guaranteed to wreck his kit each week
this is a FREE TRANSFER
but he comes with running expenses
weeks of washing shirts and shorts
socks and vests, a pair of trainers
needs to scoff huge amounts
of chips and burgers, beans and apples
pop and cola, crisps and oranges
endless packets of chewing gum.
This offer open until the end of the season
I'll have him back then
at least until the cricket starts.
Any takers?

David Harmer

15

Grandma

Grandma is teaching the trees to sing,
She's building them giant harps –
Stringing their branches with long humming wires
And painting their limbs with pictures of larks.

Grandma is teaching the cows to dance –
Sewing them evening gowns,
Sprinkling sequins along their black tails,
Waltzing them over the Downs.

Grandma is showing the frogs how to fly
High on the circus trapeze.
She swoops to the music of wild violins
Then gracefully hangs by her knees.

Jan Dean

Epitaph for the Last Martian

Crash landing caused extinction
The last of the Martian species
Here and here and here and here
He rests in pieces.

Paul Cookson

17

It's Dark in Here

I am writing these poems
From inside a lion,
And it's rather dark in here.
So please excuse the handwriting
Which may not be too clear.
But this afternoon by the lion's cage
I'm afraid I got too near.
And I'm writing these lines
From inside a lion,
And it's rather dark in here.

Shel Silverstein

18

Larks with Sharks

I love to go swimming when a great shark's about,
I tease him by tickling his tail and his snout
With the ostrich's feather I'm never without
And when I start feeling those glinty teeth close
With a scrunchy snap snap on my ankles or toes
I swim off with a laugh (for everyone knows
An affectionate nip from young sharky just shows
How dearly he loves every bit of his friend)
And when I've no leg just a stumpy chewed end
I forgive him for he doesn't mean to offend;
When he nuzzles my head, he never intends
With his teeth so delightfully set out in rows
To go further than rip off an ear or a nose,

But when a shark's feeling playful, why, anything goes!
With tears in his eyes he'll take hold of my arm
Then twist himself round with such grace and such charm
The bits slip down his throat – no need for alarm!
I've another arm left! He means me no harm!

He'll play stretch and snap with six yards of insides
The rest will wash up on the beach with the tides
What fun we've all had, what a day to remember –
Yes, a shark loves a pal he can slowly dismember.

David Orme

Granny

Through every nook and every cranny
The wind blew in on poor old Granny
Around her knees, into each ear
(And up her nose as well, I fear)

All through the night the wind grew worse
It nearly made the vicar curse
The top had fallen off the steeple
Just missing him (and other people)

It blew on man, it blew on beast
It blew on nun, it blew on priest
It blew the wig off Auntie Fanny –
But most of all, it blew on Granny!

Spike Milligan

20

Victoria's Poem

Send me upstairs without any tea,
refuse me a plaster to stick on my knee.

Make me kiss Grandpa who smells of his pipe,
make me eat beetroot, make me eat tripe.

Throw all my best dolls into the river.
Make me bacon and onions – with liver.

Tell Mr Allan I've been a bad girl,
Rename me Nellie, rename me Pearl.

But don't, even if
the world suddenly ends,
ever again, Mother,

wipe my face with a tissue
in front of my friends.

Fred Sedgwick

David and Goliath

Goliath of Gath
With hith helmet of brath
Wath theated one day
Upon the green grath.

When up thkipped thlim David
A thervant of Thaul,
And thaid I will thmite thee
Although I am tho thmall.

Thlim David thkipped down
To the edge of the thtream,
And from it'th thmooth thurfathe
Five thmooth thtoneth he took.

He loothened hith corthetth
And thevered hith head,
And all Ithreal shouted –
'Goliath ith dead!'

Anon.

Burying the Hatchet

My friend is on the warpath
because I lost his tomahawk.
I only buried it in the garden for a joke
but when I couldn't find it
he hit me with his pipe of peace.
I don't think this game is working out.

Philip Waddell

Little Miss Muffet

Little Miss Muffet sat on a tuffet,
Eating her curds and whey.
Along came a spider who sat down beside her
And said, 'Whatcha got in the bowl, sweetheart?'

Anon.

273

A Butter Bother

When Mum was making toast one day
She let my brother spread.
'You can put the butter on yourself,'
She generously said.

Well, he got some underneath his chin
He got some on his nose,
There was butter in his belly button
Butter round his toes.

He spread it quick, he spread it thick,
He coated everywhere,
It was up his arms and down his legs
It was over all his hair.

He smothered both his hands and knees,
He buttered up his face,
My brother did a thorough job
And covered every space.

Cos like a good boy always should
He did just as Mum said –
He put the butter on *himself*
Instead of on the bread!

Graham Denton

Aliens Stole My Underpants

To understand the ways
of alien beings is hard,
and I've never worked it out
why they landed in my backyard.

And I've always wondered why
on their journey from the stars,
these aliens stole my underpants
and took them back to Mars.

They came on a Monday night
when the weekend wash had been done,
pegged out on the line
to be dried by the morning sun.

Mrs Driver from next door
was a witness at the scene
when aliens snatched my underpants –
I'm glad that they were clean!

It seems they were quite choosy
as nothing else was taken.
Do aliens wear underpants
or were they just mistaken?

I think I have a theory
as to what they wanted them for,
they needed to block off a draught
blowing in through the spacecraft door.

Or maybe some Mars museum
wanted items brought back from Space.
Just think, my pair of Y-fronts
displayed in their own glass case.

And on the label beneath
would be written where they got 'em
and how such funny underwear
once covered an Earthling's bottom!

Brian Moses

Running

Above the tap it said
'Run a long time
to get hot water.'

So I ran round the room for a really long time
but I didn't get any hot water.

Michael Rosen

Little Jack Horner

Little Jack Horner
Sat in a corner,
Watching the girls go by.
Along came a beauty
And he said, 'Hi, cutie!'
And that's how he got a black eye.

Anon.

A Sumo Wrestler Chappy

A sumo wrestler chappy
One day in the ring was unhappy
   When thrown to the ground
   His mum pinned him down
And in view of the crowd changed his nappy.

Paul Cookson

The Flight of the Bumblebee

Picture this: a summer day at Grantchester.
The River Cam moves sluggish as a mollusc.
The warm air tingles with the buzz of insects
and the hum of personal stereos.
Three clever scientists are picnicking
beside a punt moored by a weeping-willow tree.

Suddenly, a bumblebee weighed down with pollen
crash-lands in a glass of chilled white wine.
One of the scientists swiftly scoops the bee
to safety, and puts it on the grass.
The bee, damp but alive, fluffs out its furry bulk.
But as it spreads its wings to dry

One of the scientists cries out: 'Great Scott! Extraordinary!
I've never noticed this before, but looking closely
at this bee, I see it's much too fat to fly!
Look at its bulk – then look at its tiny wings.'
'Why, yes!' the second scientist exclaims. 'The wings are
much too small, the body much too large!'

The third, Professor Wyatt Earp from South Bend, Indiana,
quick-draws the calculator from the holster at his hip.
He taps in figures 'Mass plus length . . . times wing-span . . .
plus the weight in grams . . . divided by the secret number
of my cash point card . . . the answer is: – Oh, wow! Oh, gee!
This bee can't fly! It's quite impossible!

'See for yourselves – we all know numbers cannot lie.'
They nod: 'You're right!' 'I'm – I'm – astounded!'
'Science demands this creature must be grounded!'
'*Bzzzzz!*' says the bee, in fluent furious bee.
'*Why don't you Bzzzz off back to your busy laboratory!*
Mind your own businesses and leave me bee!'

And then, to the scientists' dismay
a miracle occurs: it spreads its wings
it rises from the ground . . .
and flies away.

Mick Gowar

30

Dad's a Superhero

I know the truth about Dad.

Leaving our car behind (no need for it)
at the crack of dawn each day
Dad flies to the heart of the teeming metropolis.

There, clad in Superhero disguise, Dad:

supports collapsing bridges
just
in
the
nick
of time

to save thousands of terrified passengers on runaway trains,

stops hails of bullets from desperate robbers –
capturing them to the humble gratitude of the city's
overwhelmed police,

thwarts the plans of fiendish, alien, Super villains
bent on galactic domination

and rescues helpless kittens stranded up trees.

But Dad is Super modest and lets everyone think
he's just a hack on a local rag

but I know Dad's a Superhero

for no ordinary mortal could drag himself home
at the end of each working day as heroically tired as my
dad does.

Philip Waddell

31

Worst Sellers
(Books which I Probably Won't Write)

Do It Yourself Dentistry
How to Fail Every Test You'll Ever Take
Eat Yourself Fatter
The Lonely Chef – Recipes to Poison Your Friends
Caring for Your Nits
Ruin Your Life the Easy Way
The Queen – Fashion Icon and Foxy Chick
More Love Poems About a Bedside Lamp
100 Very Boring Places to Visit
Learn to Speak Spanish Really Badly in Just Eight Years

Lindsay MacRae

September

Me and My Brother

Me and my brother,
we sit up in bed
doing my dad's sayings.
I go to bed first
and I'm just dozing off
and I hear a funny voice going:
'Never let me see you doing that again,'
and it's my brother
poking his finger out just like my dad
going:
'Never let me see you doing that again.'
And so I join in
and we're both going:
'Never
let
me
see

you
doing
that
again.'

So what happens next time I get into trouble
and my dad's telling me off?
He's going:
'Never let me see you doing that again.'
So I'm looking up at my dad
going,
'Sorry, Dad, sorry.'
and I suddenly catch sight of my brother's big red
face poking out from behind my dad.

And while my dad is poking me with his finger
in time with the words:
'Never
let
me
see
you
doing
that again,'
there's my brother doing just the same
behind my dad's back
just where I can see him
and he's saying the words as well
with his mouth without making a sound.

So I start laughing
and so my dad says,
'AND IT'S NO LAUGHING MATTER.'
Of course my brother knows that one as well
and he's going with his mouth:
'And it's no laughing matter.'

But my dad's not stupid.
He knows something's going on.
So he looks round
and there's my brother
with his finger poking out
just like my dad
and I'm standing there laughing.
Oh no
then we get into
REALLY BIG TROUBLE.

Michael Rosen

Ice-Cream Poem

The chiefest of young Ethel's vices
Was eating multitudes of ices.

Whene'er the ice-van's booming tinkle
Was heard, Eth ran out in a twinkle,

And gorged herself on large 'Vanilla';
Her mum foretold that it would kill 'er

No tears could thaw her; once she ran
Away and hid inside the van,

And promptly froze upon the spot
Like the saltpillar-wife of Lot.

Poor Eth is licked! Behold the follies
Of one whose lolly went on lollies.

Though there is one thing in her favour
She now has quite a strawberry flavour

Gerda Mayer

3

Relativity

There was a young lady named Bright,
Who travelled much faster than light,
   She started one day
   In the relative way,
And returned on the previous night.

Arthur Barker

Look Out!

The witches mumble horrid chants,
You're scolded by five thousand aunts,
  A Martian pulls a fearsome face
  And hurls you into Outer Space,
You're tied in front of whistling trains,
A tomahawk has sliced your brains,
  The tigers snarl, the giants roar,
  You're sat on by a dinosaur.
In vain you're shouting 'Help' and 'Stop',
The walls are spinning like a top,
  The earth is melting in the sun
  And all the horror's just begun.
And, oh, the screams, the thumping hearts
That awful night before school starts.

Max Fatchen

Notice on a Classroom Door

FOR SALE: DARREN
Large boy, loud voice, with tidy hair (until 9.15 a.m., afterwards wild). Clean (till 11.00 a.m., then caked with mud in winter, greased with sweat in summer). Can kick a ball very hard (see classroom window).
Any reasonable offer accepted.

FOR SALE: AMANDA
Tall girl, red hair, prone to giggling. Likes music, a different group each month, and boys, a different boy each week. Usually carrying pink transparent pencil case with hearts on. Can imitate Posh Becks. And does. Often.
A bargain at 50p.

FOR SALE: PAUL
Little thoughtful chap, interested in science. Wears glasses. Ink stains on face and hands. Asks questions all day long about the dark side of Mercury, the third law of thermodynamics and the chemical table, whatever that is. Guarantees good SATs.
Will negotiate for quick sale.

FOR SALE: CHAUNTELLE
Girl who sees the funny side to everything, especially me.
Will sell to any caring class teacher. Or any uncaring one.

FOR SALE: CARL
Captain of the football team. Beckham hairdo, but can't
bend it like Beckham. Goes out currently with AMANDA
(See above). Thinks that life is essentially a midfield strategy.
Available on a free transfer.

FOR SALE: 25 other 11-year-olds, a job lot at a quid.
Includes their coats currently on the cloakroom floor, and
all unmarked lost property.

Apply as soon as possible to: Y6 teacher, _____School,
_____ton, _____shire

Please.

Fred Sedgwick

6

There Was an Art Teacher from Bude

There was an art teacher from Bude
Whose skin was completely tattooed
  From her head to her toe
  So no one would know
She taught everything in the nude

Paul Cookson

7

Postcard from Lilliput

Much news but
  little space
  on Lilliput
  cards, so use
  imagination.
  Gulliver

Debjani Chatterjee

293

I'm Glad

I'm glad the sky is painted blue,
And earth is painted green,
With such a lot of nice fresh air
All sandwiched in between.

Anon.

Come on in the Water's Lovely

Come on in the water's lovely
It isn't really cold at all
Of course you'll be quite safe up this end
If you hold tight to the wall.

Of course that fat boy there won't drown you
He's too busy drowning Gail.
Just imagine you're a tadpole.
I *know* you haven't got a tail.

Oh come on in the water's lovely
Warm and clear as anything
All the bottom tiles are squiggly
And your legs like wriggly string.

Come on in the water's lovely
It's no good freezing on the side
How do you know you're going to drown
Unless you've really tried.

What? You're really going to do it?
You'll jump in on the count of three?
Of course the chlorine doesn't blind you
Dive straight in and you'll soon see.

One – it isn't really deep at all.
Two – see just comes to my chin.
Three – oh there's the bell for closing time
And just as you jumped in!

Gareth Owen

Dad's Hiding in the Shed

Dad's hiding in the shed.
He's made me swear
Not to tell Mum
That he's hiding in there.

She was having a lie-down
With the curtains drawn.
We were playing cricket
Out on the lawn.

The scores were level.
It was really tense.
Dad had just hit a six
Right over the fence.

I bowled the next ball
As fast as I could.
Dad tried it again
As I knew he would.

But he missed and the ball
Struck him hard on the toe.
He cried out in pain
And, as he did so,

He let go of the bat.
It flew up in an arc
And crashed through the window
Where Mum lay in the dark.

Dad's hiding in the shed.
He's made me swear
Not to tell Mum
That he's hiding in there.

John Foster

A *small dragon verse*

It's not
The dragon in my plum tree
That disturbs me,
I confess.
But all day long
The plaintive cries
Of damsons in distress.

Paul Bright

12

My Mates

Jimmy Greenwood kisses slugs.
I've seen him.
He'll let you look for 50p.
He puts one on his hand
pushes out his lips
shuts his eyes (nearly)
and lays a smacker on its face.
When he pulls his lips away
they're covered in slime
and he licks it off.

He loves them.
If he could, he'd marry a slug.
One of the big fat black ones
or the long, streaky brown ones.

He calls them 'darling'
'dearest' and 'sweetie pie'.
I've heard him.
It's only 20p to listen.
He puts his mouth right up
to where he thinks their ear is
and whispers.

He even takes them to bed with him.
He puts them inside his 'jamas
and lets them slither over his belly.
So he says.

I've got 20p left.
I'm off to watch Alan Wright
push woodlice up his nose.

Gus Grenfell

Shoem*

Time flizzes when I'm wrizzing –
some words are toomely long,
and so I merge and jummix
to squeet them in my song.

It's really not too diffcky
to get my words to scrush –
saves tromoil and timassle,
when in a hurrid rush.

300

There's only one small difflem
for my puzzizzy head –
I'm baffplussed and conboozled
by what it is I said!

*Short Poem

Flizzes = flies and whizzes

Toomely = too and extremely

Squeet = squeeze and fit

Scrush = squash and crush

Timassle = time and hassle

Difflem = Difficulty and problem

Baffplussed = baffled and nonplussed

Wrizzing = busy and writing

Jummix = jumble and mix

Diffcky = difficult and tricky

Tromoil = trouble and turmoil

Hurrid = hurried and horrid

Puzzizzy = puzzled and dizzy

Conboozled = confused and bamboozled

Liz Brownlee

The Mermaid

Say not the mermaid is a myth,
I knew one once named Mrs Smith.
She stood while playing cards or knitting:
Mermaids are not equipped for sitting.

Ogden Nash

15

Hunter Trials

It's awf'lly bad luck on Diana,
  Her ponies have swallowed their bits;
She fished down their throats with a spanner
  And frightened them all into fits.

So now she's attempting to borrow.
  Do lend her some bits, Mummy, *do*;
I'll lend her my own for to-morrow,
  But to-day *I*'ll be wanting them too.

Just look at Prunella on Guzzle,
  The wizardest pony on earth;
Why doesn't she slacken his muzzle
  And tighten the breech in his girth?

I say, Mummy, there's Mrs Geyser
  And doesn't she look pretty sick?
I bet it's because Mona Lisa
  Was hit on the hock with a brick.

Miss Blewitt says Monica threw it,
   But Monica says it was Joan,
And Joan's very thick with Miss Blewitt,
   So Monica's sulking alone.

And Margaret failed in her paces,
   Her withers got tied in a noose,
So her coronets caught in the traces
   And now all her fetlocks are loose.

Oh, it's me now. I'm terribly nervous.
   I wonder if Smudges will shy.
She's practically certain to swerve as
   Her Pelham is over one eye.

* * *

Oh wasn't it naughty of Smudges?
   Oh, Mummy, I'm sick with disgust.
She threw me in front of the Judges,
   And my silly old collarbone's bust.

Sir John Betjeman

16

He Spoke the Truth

'Your teeth are like the stars,' he said
And pressed her hand so white.
He spoke the truth for, like the stars,
Her teeth came out at night.

Anon.

Cat Message

Shemu the cat
Whose ancestors
Prowled amongst the pyramids
Today received a special visitor

Neferhotep
Ambassador
From the constellation of Orion

Upon Neferhotep's
Departure
Shemu tried her best
To warn her mistress
Of Neferhotep's message

The Earth is about to be invaded

Shemu lay on the carpet
And made letter shapes
With her body
I – N – V – A – S – I – O – N

Shemu brought twigs and scraps of bark
Into the kitchen
Arranged in the symbol O-ki-hran
Which is Orionese for
You are about to be invaded by hideous aliens
From the constellation Andromeda

Shemu even reprogrammed the video
To play Star Trek tapes

But Shemu's only reward
For her efforts
Was some tinned cat-food

Humans, thought Shemu,
Can be so . . .
Dumb

Roger Stevens

18

Miss Creedle Teaches Creative Writing

'This morning,' cries Miss Creedle,
'We're all going to use our imaginations,
We're going to close our eyes 3W and imagine.
Are we ready to imagine, Darren?
I'm going to count to three.
At one, we wipe our brains completely clean;
At two, we close our eyes;
And at three, we imagine.
Are we all imagining? Good.
Here is a piece of music by Beethoven to help us.
Beethoven's dates were 1770 to 1827.
(See The Age of Revolutions in your History books.)
Although Beethoven was deaf and a German
He wrote many wonderful symphonies,
But this was a long time before anyone of us was born.
Are you imagining a time before you were born?
What does it look like? Is it dark?
(Embryo is a good word you might use.)
Does the music carry you away like a river?
What is the name of the river? Can you smell it?
Foetid is an exciting adjective.
As you float down the river
Perhaps you land on an alien planet.

Tell me what sounds you hear.
If there are incredible monsters
Tell me what they look like but not now.
(Your book entitled *Tackle Pre-History This Way*
Will be of assistance here.)
Perhaps you are cast adrift in a broken barrel
In stormy shark-infested waters
(Remember the work we did on piranhas for RE?)
Try to see yourself. Can you do that?
See yourself at the bottom of a pothole in the Andes
With both legs broken
And your life ebbing away inexorably.
What does the limestone feel like?
See the colours.
Have you done that? Good.
And now you may open your eyes.

Your imagining time is over,
Now it is writing time.
Are we ready to write? Good.
Then write away.
Wayne, you're getting some exciting ideas down.
Tracy, that's lovely.
Darren, you haven't written anything.
Couldn't you put the date?
You can't think of anything to write.
Well, what did you see when you closed your eyes?
But you must have seen something besides the black.
Yes, apart from the little squiggles.
Just the black. I see.
Well, try to think
Of as many words for black as you can.'

Miss Creedle whirls about the class
Like a benign typhoon
Spinning from one quailing homestead to another.
I dream of peaceful ancient days
In Mr Swindell's class
When the hours passed like a dream
Filled with order and measuring and tests.
Excitement is not one of the things I come to school for.
I force my eyes shut
But all I see
Is a boy of twelve
Sitting at a desk one dark November day
Writing his poem.
And Darren is happy to discover
There is only one word for black
And that will have to suffice
Until the bell rings for all of us.

Gareth Owen

Diary of Jack

Monday
Took Jill out.
Went up a hill.
Fell down the hill.
Put vinegar on my head
Also, some brown paper.

Peter Dixon

Diary of Jill

Tuesday
Jack took me out for a drink yesterday.
Jack fell down
He put some vinegar on his head.
Also, some brown paper.
Jack is a twit.
I will not go out with him again.

Peter Dixon

Coathanger

I gave my love a coathanger,
She flung it back at me.
It acted like a boomerang
And hit her on the knee.

Colin West

The Pong

It might have come from Peter,
It might have come from Dean,
But when they stood together
It was sort of in between.

It smelt a bit like armpits,
It smelt a bit like feet,
And if either walked away
It was sort of incomplete.

John Mole

23

I Would Win the Gold if These Were Olympic Sports . . .

Bubble gum blowing
Goggle box watching
Late morning snoring
Homework botching

Quilt ruffling
Little brother teasing
Pizza demolishing
Big toe cheesing

Insult hurling, wobbly throwing
Infinite blue belly button fluff growing

Late night endurance computer screen gazing
Non-attentive open-jawed eyeball glazing

Ultimate volume decibel blaring
Long-distance marathon same sock wearing

Recognize all these as sports then meet
Me! The Champ Apathetic Athlete!

Paul Cookson

24

Poem Spoken by a Cat to Its Owner's Friends Who are Flat-sitting

I have eaten
the chicken
you had on the sideboard
defrosting

and which you were hoping
to roast
and serve with wine
to your friends

forgive me
I'm a cat
we have no manners
we're always like that

Matthew Sweeney

25

The Pupil Control Gadget

Science teacher Robert West
built a gadget which, when pressed,
caused consternation far and wide
by zapping pupils in mid stride.
It froze all motion, stopped all noise,
controlled the rowdy girls and boys,
and on fast forward was great fun.
It made them get their schoolwork done,
their hands a blur, their paper smoking,
with teachers cheering, laughing, joking.
And on rewind (that, too, was nice)
you could make them do their
    schoolwork twice.
Robert, now a millionaire
is selling gadgets everywhere.
Timid teachers, pupil bossed
pay cash and never mind the cost.

Marian Swinger

History Lesson: Part Two – The Romans

All over their Empire
the Romans built impressive buildings
such as forts, villas and monuments.
In big cities they constructed huge *Amphitheatres*
where great games and spectacles were held.

The best known of these
are the Roman Games with contests,
often to the death, between animals,
between men and between women combatants.

It was in one of these amphitheatres
that Miranda, the wife of Emperor Tiberius Tempus,
accidentally fell from her balcony into the arena
and was attacked and eaten by a tiger.

The tiger was told off and sent to bed.
Everyone agreed it was bad he ate her,
and now the Emperor was sad he ate her,
and poor old Miranda was mad he ate her,
but the tiger said she was tasty and he was
GLADIATOR!

John Rice

27

Little Red Riding Hood and the Wolf

As soon as Wolf began to feel
That he would like a decent meal,
He went and knocked on Grandma's door.
When Grandma opened it, she saw
The sharp white teeth, the horrid grin,
And Wolfie said, 'May I come in?'
Poor Grandmamma was terrified,
'He's going to eat me up!' she cried.
And she was absolutely right.
He ate her up in one big bite.
But Grandmamma was small and tough,
And Wolfie wailed, 'That's not enough!
I haven't yet begun to feel
That I have had a decent meal!'
He ran around the kitchen yelping,
'I've *got* to have another helping!'
Then added with a frightful leer,
'I'm therefore going to wait right here
Till Little Miss Red Riding Hood
Comes home from walking in the wood.'

He quickly put on Grandma's clothes.
(Of course he hadn't eaten those.)
He dressed himself in coat and hat.
He put on shoes and after that
He even brushed and curled his hair,
Then sat himself in Grandma's chair.
In came the little girl in red.
She stopped. She stared. And then she said,

'*What great big ears you have, Grandma.*'
'*All the better to hear you with,*' the Wolf replied.
'*What great big eyes you have, Grandma,*' said Little Red
    Riding Hood.
'*All the better to see you with,*' the Wolf replied.

He sat there watching her and smiled.
He thought, I'm going to eat this child.
Compared with her old Grandmamma
She's going to taste like caviar.

Then Little Red Riding Hood said, '*But Grandma,
what a lovely great big furry coat you have on.*'

'That's wrong!' cried Wolf. 'Have you forgot
To tell me what BIG TEETH I've got?
Ah well, no matter what you say,
I'm going to eat you anyway.'
The small girl smiles. One eyelid flickers.
She whips a pistol from her knickers.
She aims it at the creature's head
And *bang bang bang*, she shoots him dead.
A few weeks later, in the wood,
I came across Miss Riding Hood.
But what a change! No cloak of red,
No silly hood upon her head.
She said, 'Hello, and do please note
My lovely furry WOLFSKIN COAT.'

Roald Dahl

Robinson Crusoe's Wise Sayings

You can never have too many turtle's eggs.
I'm the most interesting person in this room.
A beard is as long as I want it to be.

The swimmer on his own doesn't need trunks.
A tree is a good clock.
If you talk to a stone long enough you'll fall asleep.

I know it's Christmas because I cry.
Waving at ships is useless.
Footprints make me happy, unless they're my own.

Ian McMillan

The Optimist

The optimist fell ten storeys
  And at each window bar
He shouted to the folks inside
  'Doing all right so far!'

Anon.

Dragon Love Poem

When you smile
the room lights up

and I have to call
the fire brigade

Roger Stevens

October

An Epicure Dining at Crewe

An epicure dining at Crewe
Once found a large mouse in his stew.
  Said the waiter, 'Don't shout
  And wave it about,
Or the rest will be wanting one, too!'

Anon.

The Red Herring

There was once a high wall, a bare wall. And
against this wall, there was a ladder,
a long ladder. And on the ground,
under the ladder, was a red
herring, a dry red herring.

And then a man came along. And in his hands
(they were dirty hands) this man had
a heavy hammer, a long nail,
(it was also a sharp nail) and
a ball of string. A thick ball of string.

All right. So the man climbed up
the ladder (right up to the top)
and knocked in the sharp nail:
spluk! Just like that.
Right on the top of the wall. The bare wall.

Then he dropped the hammer. It dropped
right down to the ground. And on to the nail
he tied a piece of string, a long
piece of string, and on to the string
he tied the red herring. The dry red herring.

And let it drop. And then he climbed
down the ladder (right down
to the bottom), picked up the hammer
and also the ladder (which was pretty heavy)
and went off. A long way off.

And since then, that red herring, the dry
red herring on the end of the string, which is
quite a long piece, has been
very, very slowly swinging and
swinging to a stop. A full stop.

I expect you wonder why I made
up this story, such a simple story. Well
I did it just to annoy people.
Serious people. And perhaps also
to amuse children. Small children.

George Macbeth

Blow-Dry Bill's a Baddie

Blow-Dry Bill's a baddie
A hairdresser by trade
But at weekends he dons a mask
And does the odd bank raid.

He doesn't take a gun with him
No bullets does he fire
Instead he takes a trusty friend
An old sawn-off hair drier.

'How threatening can a hair drier be?'
I hear you people say
Well, if the staff don't give him cash
He blows them all away.

Richard Caley

My Uncle Percy Once Removed

My Uncle Percy once removed
his bobble hat, scarf, overcoat,
woolly jumper, string vest,
flared trousers and purple Y-fronts
and ran on to the pitch at Wembley
during a Cup Final
and was at once removed
by six stewards and nine officers of the law.
Once they'd caught him.

Paul Cookson

Please Mrs Butler

Please Mrs Butler
This boy Derek Drew
Keeps copying my work, Miss.
What shall I do?

Go and sit in the hall, dear.
Go and sit in the sink.
Take your books on the roof, my lamb.
Do whatever you think.

Please Mrs Butler
This boy Derek Drew
Keeps taking my rubber, Miss.
What shall I do?

Keep it in your hand, dear.
Hide it up your vest.
Swallow it if you like, my love.
Do what you think best.

Please Mrs Butler
This boy Derek Drew
Keeps calling me rude names, Miss.
What shall I do?

Lock yourself in the cupboard, dear.
Run away to sea.
Do whatever you can, my flower.
But *don't ask me!*

Allan Ahlberg

As I Was Standing in the Street

As I was standing in the street,
    As quiet as could be,
A great big ugly man came up
    And tied his horse to me.

Anon.

My Old Man

My old man's a pilot
He steers a big starship
He wears white plastic trousers
And his food comes through a drip.

My old mum's a robot
Her joints are made of tin
She's covered with washable velvet
And she answers to the name of Lyn.

My teacher's a dalek
He has a boring voice
He likes to wave his wand at you
And exterminate the boys.

My sister's an alien
Dad found her growing on Mars
She won't touch peas and carrots
'Cos she lives on chocolate bars.

My friends think I'm peculiar
Because my ears are green.
If they saw what I can turn into
They'd scream and scream and scream.

Angela Topping

One Fine Day in the Middle of the Night

One fine day in the middle of the night
Two dead men got up to fight
Back to back they faced each other,
Drew their swords and shot each other.

Anon.

Miss! Sue Is Kissing

Miss! Sue is kissing
the tadpoles again.
She is, Miss. I did,
I asked her. She said
something about catching
him young. Getting one
her own age. I don't know,
Miss. She keeps whispering
'Prince, Prince.' Isn't that
a dog's name, Miss?

Michael Harrison

10

Wellingtons

I love the wild wet winter days
Of rain and slushy sleet
For it's then I fetch my Welligons
I mean my rubber Gellibongs
Oh dear I mean my Webbingtons
And pull them on my feet.

My sister Jane hates rainy days
The cold makes Mary cry
But me I've got my Wellinbots
Oh dear I mean my Bellingwots
No no I mean my Welltingots
To keep me warm and dry.

But isn't it a nuisance
Isn't it a shame
That though I love you Wellibongs
I just can't say your name.

Gareth Owen

Thirty Days Hath September

Thirty days hath September,
And the rest I can't remember.

Michael Rosen

Doctor Emmanuel

Doctor Emmanuel Harrison-Hyde
Has a very big head with brains inside.
I wonder what happens inside the brains
That Doctor Emmanuel's head contains.

James Reeves

13

First Love

Everyone says that my girlfriend Gemma
Is big for her age
And that what we apparently feel for each other
Is only a stage.

But what, when they grumble, I have to agree
Is as plain as day
Is that Gemma tends to throw her big weight about
Every which way.

Once when I showed her a shed in our garden
She climbed on the roof
And then when I wasn't expecting leapt down like an
    Amazon.
Strewth!

All of my breath was completely knocked out of me,
All of my puff,
But just to have Gemma landing on top of me
Was enough.

John Mole

Stinker

Poor old Stinker's dead and gone
We'll see his face no more
For what he thought was H_2O
Was H_2SO_4.

Anon.

When I'm Older

I'll never pull my socks up. I'll never fold my clothes
I'll even have a servant to wipe my drippy nose
And at the dinner table FIRST I'll have my sweet
I'll always rush my tea and never brush my teeth

I'll never wipe my face and never clean my shoes
I'll never cry never ever. I'll never flush the loo
I'll never do my homework. I'll never eat sprouts
When Mum asks, 'where you going' I'll say 'OUT'

I'll never clean my bedroom, never change my socks
I'll always yell 'OI!' through the letterbox
I'll never wash the pots. I'll never do my bed.
For breakfast I'll only eat jam on shortbread

I'll never wipe my feet, I'll never wipe my nose
I'll never cut my nails and I'll never wash my clothes
I'll always ring the doorbell, I'll never wear a tie
I'll always answer the telephone with the word
                                              Goodbye!

Lemn Sissay

Scatterbrain

Before he goes to bed at night
Scatterbrained Uncle Pat
Gives the clock a saucer of milk
And winds up the tabby cat.

Gareth Owen

Seasick

'I don't feel whelk,' whaled the squid, sole-fully.
'What's up?' asked the doctopus.
'I've got sore mussels and a tunny-hake,' she told him.

'Lie down and I'll egg salmon you,' mermaid the doctopus.
'Rays your voice,' said the squid. 'I'm a bit hard of herring.'
'Sorry! I didn't do it on porpoise,' replied the doctopus orc-
  wardly.

He helped her to oyster self on to his couch
And asked her to look up so he could sea urchin.
He soon flounder plaice that hurt.

'This'll make it eel,' he said, whiting a prescription.
'So I won't need to see the sturgeon?' she asked.
'Oh, no,' he told her. 'In a couple of dace you'll feel brill.'

'Cod bless you,' she said.
'That'll be sick squid,' replied the doctopus.

Nick Toczek

18

Lost Voice

Our teacher lost her voice
today . . .
 We don't know where it's gone,
we've searched all round the classroom
and all round the hall.

We've searched inside the cupboard,
we've looked behind the wall
and even in the toilets . . .
 It can't be found at all!

My mother says it's dreadful
my mother says it's sad . . .
 Miss Johnson only
 whispers
 But we are rather glad.

Peter Dixon

The Monster

Some are ugly,
Some are tall,
Some are scary,
Some are small.
Some are difficult to see.
And some are in my family.

Emma Hjeltnes

The Old Man of Blackheath

There was an old man of Blackheath
Who sat on a set of false teeth.
    Said he, with a start,
    'O, Lord, bless my heart!
I have bitten myself underneath!'

Anon.

21

It Makes Dad Mad

Let's ransack the toy box,
Cos it makes Dad mad.
Let's squeeze jelly in our socks,
Cos it makes Dad mad.
Let's wrestle in the flower beds,
And pour the compost on our heads;
Let's lock the dog in the garden shed,
Cos it makes Dad mad.

Let's spread toothpaste on the telly,
Cos it makes Dad mad.
Let's pour rhubarb in our wellies,
Cos it makes Dad mad.
Let's burst a bag of flour,
And put frogspawn in the shower;
Let's just scream for half an hour,
Cos it makes Dad mad.

Let's stamp in muddy puddles,
Cos it makes Dad mad.
Let's fill the bathroom up with bubbles,
Cos it makes Dad mad.
Let's tip treacle on the cat,
And chase it with a cricket bat;
Let's cut up the front door mat,
Cos it makes Dad mad.

Dad's asleep, don't wake him up.
The room's a mess, but we'll scrape it up.
He'll want some tea, so we'll make a cup.
Quiet – you can hear him snore,
He won't mind the sugar on the floor,
And all the milk spilt up the wall . . .
Watch the carpet – don't you fall!
What did you go and do that for?
COS IT MAKES DAD MAD!!

Dave Ward

22

I Love to Do My Homework

I love to do my homework
I never miss a day.
I even love the men in white
Who are taking me away.

Anon.

Elephantasy

'There's been an elephant in my fridge,'
  I heard an old man mutter.
'How can you tell?' I asked him.
  'Footprints in the butter!'

'The elephant's still in there.'
  The old man gave a 'Tut!'
'How do you know?' I asked him.
  'Look, the door won't shut!'

Celia Warren

24

Whether the Weather

Whether the weather be fine
Or whether the weather be not
Whether the weather be cold
Or whether the weather be hot –
We'll weather the weather
Whatever the weather
Whether we like it or not!

Anon.

Words Behaving Badly

Words
Develop nasty habits –
Getting out of order,
Going off at tangents,
Breaking rules,
Attention seeking.
Give them fifty lines.
They take delight
In ambushing the reader,
Going round in gangs
With their unsuitable friends
Imagining they're poems!
Words –
I'd keep an eye on them
If I were you.

Sue Cowling

A Dog's Day

Every dog
Will have his day.
On my dog's day
He ran away.

Roger Stevens

Black Socks

Black socks, they never get dirty,
The longer you wear them the stronger they get.
Sometimes I think I should wash them,
But something inside me keeps saying,
'Not yet, not yet, not yet, not yet, not yet.'

Anon.

My Sister Sybil

Sipping soup, my sister Sybil
Seems inclined to drool and dribble.
If it wasn't for this foible,
Meal-times would be more enjoible!

Colin West

Bug in a Jug

Curious fly,
Vinegary jug.
Slippery edge,
Pickled bug.

Anon.

Ghoul School Rules

1. Glide, don't flit!
2. Keep your head ON at all times.
3. No clanking of chains between lessons.
4. No walking through walls. Wait OUTSIDE the classroom.
5. No skeletons to be taken out of cupboards.
6. Line up QUIETLY for the ghost train at the end of the night.

Sue Cowling

31

The Ghoul Inspectre's Coming

The Ghoul
Inspectre's coming,
dust off your lazy bones –
tidy out your coffins, polish
up your mournful moans.
Practise rib cage rattles,
check that your chains still clank, gibber when you're
spoken to and keep your cellars dank. Display your
bat collection and cobweb hanging talents –
freshen up the bloodstains, see
that the spook books balance.
Hover to attention, grease
your glides and brush
your mould – the
Ghoul Inspectre's
coming, make
sure his
welcome's
Cold!

Liz Brownlee

November

Diary of Cock Robin

Saturday
  Went to Saturday flying club
  Met Sparrow.
  Sparrow showed me his new bow and arrow
  Sparrow shot me.

Peter Dixon

Escape Plan

As I, Stegosaurus,
stand motionless
in the museum
I am secretly planning
my escape.

At noon
Tyrannosaurus Rex
will cause a diversion
by wheeling around the museum's high ceilings
and diving at the curators and museum staff
while I
quietly slip out of the fire exit
and melt
into the London crowds.

Roger Stevens

3

A Poem for My Cat

You're black and sleek and beautiful
What a pity your best friends won't tell you
Your breath smells of Kit-E-Kat.

Adrian Henri

The Hungry Wolf

The hungry wolf
  is very wild
and is guaranteed
  to devour a child.

So do take care
  if a wolf's about,
and if you fancy chips,
  send your sister out!

John Rice

Timetable

First-year ghosts, 9 p.m.,
First class, 'Elementary Moaning,'
10 p.m. at local churchyard,
'Get to Grips with Graveyard Groaning,'
10.30, practical,
'How to Remove your Head,'
12 midnight, back to churchyard,
'Seven Steps to Wake the Dead,'
1 a.m., 'Dragging Chains,'
2 a.m., 'Ringing Bells,'
3 a.m., 'To Mix Fake Blood,'
4 a.m., 'Revolting Smells,'
5 a.m., dawn instructions,
'Murky Mists and Spooky Lighting,'
5.30, theory class,
'The Basics of Successful Frightening,'
6 a.m., lost property,
Please reclaim your missing head,
6.30, class dismissed,
Vanish, fade or float to bed.

Julia Rawlinson

Hindsight

Yesterday
I went to get my hindsight tested.
It was perfect.
Looking back,
I should have known that.

Andy Seed

A Dream

I dreamed a dream next Tuesday week,
Beneath the apple-trees;
I thought my eyes were big pork-pies,
And my nose was Stilton cheese.

The clock struck twenty minutes to six,
When a frog sat on my knee;
I asked him to lend me eighteen pence
But he borrowed a shilling of me.

Anon.

A Piglet

I'm a piglet, pink and stout.
If I'm cold, I sneeze and sniff.
If I have to blow my snout,
I take out my oinkerchief.

Jack Prelutsky

9

Kate

In the kitchen Kate went tripping
Landing in a vat of dripping.
When the Red Cross came to fetch her,
Kate kept slipping off the stretcher.

Colin West

10

On the Bridge at Midnight

She stood on the bridge at midnight,
Her limbs were all a-quiver.
She gave a cough, her leg fell off,
And floated down the river.

Anon.

11

Sardines

You slip behind your parents' clothes
  in nineteen sixty-eight,
pull shut the wardrobe door, then
  curl into a ball.
                    You wait.

It's very still in there. So quiet.
  Your chin rests on your knees.
A long fur-coat is tickling
  so much you want to sneeze.

A year goes by. Neil Armstrong walks
  the surface of the moon
as slow as honey, while you think
  'Someone will find me soon!'

You fiddle with your father's ties.
  The earth crawls round the sun
and footsteps pass the wardrobe door.
  – It could be anyone!

The world outside turns decimal
and all the old coins go
the way of dinosaurs, of early
morning mist, of snow.

It's very quiet in there. So still.
Your knees support your chin
while you whisper, 'Any minute now
someone will burst in . . .'

Fashions change: hemlines fall and rise.
Hands sometimes reach inside
to take a shirt or dress away –
the door is opened wide

and then it's closed, and then it's dark
once more. Leaves grow. Leaves fall.
The earth crawls round the sun again.
(You almost *hear* it crawl.)

One day in nineteen eighty-five
you think about your life
alone; but there's room for neither
children nor a wife

in there. It's very still. So quiet.
Your chin rests on your knees.
Sometimes you whistle in that dark
like wind through broken trees.

'No one's going to find,' you say,
　'my perfect hiding-place.
Not now.' It's nineteen ninety-nine.
　The planet spins through space,

the trees grow fat with overcoats
　and you, you droop until
(at last) you fall asleep.
　　　　　　　　　Good night.
It's quiet in there, and still.
So still.
　　　So very still.

Stephen Knight

The Painting Lesson

'What's THAT, dear?'
asked the new teacher.

'It's Mummy,' I replied.

'But mums aren't green and orange!
You really haven't TRIED.
You don't just paint in SPLODGES
– You're old enough to know
You need to THINK before you work . . .
Now – have another go.'

She helped me draw two arms and legs,
A face with sickly smile,
A rounded body, dark brown hair,
A hat – and, in a while,
She stood back (with her face bright pink):
'That's SO much better – don't you think?'

But she turned white
At ten to three
When an orange-green blob
Collected me.

'Hi, Mum!'

Trevor Harvey

13

Assembly

We assemble.
That's why it's called
assembly.
We sit cross-legged.
The area of the bottom
multiplied by the number of pupils
is greater than the area
of the hall floor.
We squiggle, we squeeze,
we squash, we squabble.
Jamie is asked to stay behind.
Behind is another word for bottom.
Miss walks on the stage.
So does Miss, Miss, Sir,
Miss, Sir, Miss, Miss and
Miss.

We have a talk about being good.
It is good to be good.
It is bad to be bad.
We will all be good.
We sing a song about trees.
The bone in my bottom
cuts into the floorboards.
I'm not worried about the floorboards.
Miss reads out the notices
but nobody notices.
We stand up.
I pull my bottom bone
out of the floorboards.
We line up like soldiers,
like prisoners, like refugees.
We file out
in a sensible manner.
The hall is now empty.
Except for Jamie.

Steve Turner

14

The Blunderblat

Until I saw the Blunderblat
I doubted its existence;
But late last night with Vera White,
I saw one in the distance.

I reached for my binoculars,
Which finally I focused;
I watched it rise into the skies,
Like some colossal locust.

I heard it hover overhead,
I shrieked as it came nearer;
I held my breath, half scared to death,
And prayed it might take Vera.

And so it did, I'm glad to say,
Without too much resistance.
Dear Blunderblat, I'm sorry that
I doubted your existence.

Colin West

Two Lists

I'm going out now
To the shops for my dad

I've got two lists
One of things to buy

Carrots
Peas
Bread
An apple pie

One of things to remember:

Don't talk to strangers
Go straight there
Be careful crossing the roads
Don't talk to strangers
Come straight back
Don't lose the money
Don't talk to strangers
Don't get lost
Don't forget the change

And Tommy . . .

Yes, dad?

Don't talk to strangers

I'm back now from going
To the shops for my dad.

I didn't talk to strangers
I went straight there
I was careful crossing the roads
I didn't talk to strangers
I came straight back
I didn't lose the money
I didn't talk to strangers
I didn't get lost
I didn't forget the change
And . . . I didn't talk to strangers

So what did you forget?
Dad said

The carrots
The peas
The apple pie
And . . .

Yes?

The bread

Tony Bradman

My Knickers

My knickers are enormous
My knickers are supreme
They cover nearly all of me
In lovely bottle-green

The gusset's made of iron
The waist is made of plastic
And Martin Cooper likes to twang
Their re-inforced elastic

Compared to other knickers
My knickers are the best
They reach to well below my knees
And just above my chest

My knickers are so versatile
And truly heaven-sent
For when I go out camping
I use them as a tent

My knickers are unusual
And sometimes for a change
I like to wear them on my head
Which looks a little strange

Once travelling on a cruise ship
Which sank just off Peru
We used my knickers as the boat
For passengers and crew

My knickers are remarkable
And have a special function:
To be as big as Birmingham
Without Spaghetti Junction

Completely indestructible
With girders round the back
They can withstand a hurricane
Or nuclear attack

Recognized by royalty
For quality and size
My knickers have been knighted
They've won the Nobel Prize

Though other knickers come and go
And fall along the way
My knickers are immortal
My knickers never fray

Ann Ziety

The Giggles

Alexandra Daunton-Diggle
Was swallowed by a giant giggle
Which started gently at her toes
And finished just above her nose

No one saw, no one heard
It came and went without a word
Gobbling her whole (plus party frock)
It spat out one white cotton sock

All sniggerers should have a care
That giggles take you unawares
And that no matter what you do
They always get the better of you

Lindsay MacRae

18

My Spaniel

I've been teaching my spaniel to play
The piano this many a day,
But his Mozart's a curse
And his Bach is much worse
Than his bite, I am sorry to say.

Gerard Benson

19

Two Witches Discuss Good Grooming

'How do you keep your teeth so green
Whilst mine remain so white?
Although I rub them vigorously
With cold slime every night.

'Your eyes are such a lovely shade
Of bloodshot, streaked with puce.
I prod mine daily with a stick
But it isn't any use.

'I envy so the spots and boils
That brighten your complexion.
Even rat spit on my face
Left no trace of infection.

'I've even failed to have bad breath
After eating sewage raw,
Yet your halitosis
Can strip paint from a door.'

'My dear, there is no secret,
Now I don't mean to brag.
What you see is nature's work
I'm just a natural hag.'

John Coldwell

20

The Sweet

I've found a sweet
In my jeans' pocket
It could be a toffee
Or what's left
Of a sherbet rocket.

It's all covered
In fluff and other stuff
And stuck to some stones
I found in the street
But it's still a sweet.

Scrape off the fluff
And the slime
And all that stuff
Till it looks almost clean

And just
Pop it in.

Tony Bradman

Nine Reasons for Hating Children

Their coats all over
    the cloakroom floor,
their fondness for
    the open door.

The way they chatter,
    the way they chew.
I really hate them.
    Look. Don't you?

The Velcro crackling
    on their Nikes
The way they career
    about on bikes.

Some children, I know,
    look like roses . . .
but they pick their ears
    and pick their noses

and others, though
   told time and again,
don't wash their hands
   or pull the chain.

Many children
   I have sighted
still support (NO!)
   Man United!

Kids may look good
   but run a mile
when you see one.
   They are vile.

Fred Sedgwick

Flares

I wear flares
And am often catapulted
Into the night sky
Where I drift slowly down
My legs brilliantly glowing
Lighting up the town

Roger Stevens

Twin Trouble

Una and Ursula,
Identical twins,
Can't tell them apart,
They're alike as two pins.

They'll tell you that Una
Parts her hair on the right,
And then you'll discover
It's changed overnight.
'This one's me,' says Ursula,
'My ribbon's red;'
But next day she'll trick you
With a green one instead.
They tease all the teachers
By changing their places,
And even their parents
Look hard at both faces.
'I'm me . . . ME!' says Ursula.
'You're not! You are YOU,
And I'm ME!' declares Una,
'I'm Me through and through!'
Then they say 'We're two U's
With UNUSUAL names,
And we love to confuse YOU
With our tricks, jokes and games!'
'We are US!' they agree,
'As alike as two pins,
Una and Ursula,
Identical twins!'

Anne Harvey

Sorry Sorry Sorry

Sorry, I wasn't listening
to a single word you said
I drifted off into the mist
that grew inside my head

Sorry, I wasn't listening
I didn't hear a sound:
I went where dreams of dreams have dreams
and sky and ground swap round

Sorry, I wasn't listening
aliens were at the door
asking for directions
to the planet XR4

Sorry, I wasn't listening
some pirates came for me
first I had to walk the plank
and then I made them tea

Sorry – I wasn't listening
I don't know what went on
could you say it one more time –
hang on – where've you gone?

James Carter

The Dragon in the Cellar

There's a dragon!
There's a dragon!
There's a dragon in the cellar!
Yeah, we've got a cellar-dweller.
There's a dragon in the cellar.

He's a cleanliness fanatic,
takes his trousers and his jacket
to the dragon from the attic
who puts powder by the packet
in a pre-set automatic
with a rattle and a racket
that's disturbing and dramatic.

There's a dragon!
There's a dragon!
There's a dragon in the cellar
with a flame that's red 'n' yeller.
There's a dragon in the cellar . . .

. . . and a dragon on the roof
who's only partly waterproof,
so she's borrowed an umbrella
from the dragon in the cellar.

There's a dragon!
There's a dragon!
There's a dragon in the cellar!
If you smell a panatella
it's the dragon in the cellar.

And the dragon from the study's
helping out his cellar buddy,
getting wet and soap-suddy
with the dragon from the loo
there to give a hand too,
while the dragon from the porch
supervises with a torch.
Though the dragon from the landing,
through a slight misunderstanding,
is busy paint-stripping and sanding.

There's a dragon!
There's a dragon!
There's a dragon in the cellar!
Find my dad, and tell the feller
there's a dragon in the cellar . . .

. . . where the dragon from my room
goes zoom, zoom, zoom
in a cloud of polish and spray-perfume,
cos he's the dragon whom
they pay to brighten up the gloom
with a mop and a duster and a broom, broom, broom.

There's a dragon!
There's a dragon!
There's a dragon in the cellar!
Gonna get my mum and tell her
there's a dragon in the cellar.

Nick Toczek

The Owl and the Pussy-Cat

The Owl and the Pussy-Cat went to sea
In a beautiful pea-green boat,
They took some honey, and plenty of money,
Wrapped up in a five-pound note.
The Owl looked up to the stars above,
And sang to a small guitar,
'O lovely Pussy! O Pussy, my love,
What a beautiful Pussy you are,
You are,
You are!
What a beautiful Pussy you are!'

Pussy said to the Owl, 'You elegant fowl!
How charmingly sweet you sing!
O let us be married! too long have we tarried:
But what shall we do for a ring?'
They sailed away, for a year and a day,
To the land where the Bong-tree grows,
And there in a wood a Piggy-wig stood
With a ring at the end of his nose,
His nose,
His nose,
With a ring at the end of his nose.

'Dear Pig, are you willing to sell for one shilling
  Your ring?' Said the Piggy, 'I will.'
So they took it away, and were married next day
  By the Turkey who lives on the hill.
They dined on mince, and slices of quince,
  Which they ate with a runcible spoon;
And hand in hand, on the edge of the sand,
  They danced by the light of the moon,
    The moon,
    The moon,
  They danced by the light of the moon.

Edward Lear

Horace

Much to his Mum and Dad's dismay
Horace ate himself one day.
He didn't stop to say his grace,
He just sat down and ate his face.
'We can't have this!' his Dad declared,
'If that lad's ate, he should be shared.'
But even as he spoke they saw
Horace eating more and more:
First his legs, and then his thighs,
His arms, his nose, his hair, his eyes . . .
'Stop him, someone!' Mother cried,
'Those eyeballs would be better fried!'
But all too late! And now the silly
Had even started on his willy!
'Oh foolish child!' the father mourns,
'You could have deep-fried that with prawns,
Some parsley and some tartare sauce . . .'
But H. was on his second course:
His liver and his lights and lung,
His ears, his neck, his chin, his tongue . . .
'To think I raised him from the cot,
And now he's going to scoff the lot!'

His Mother cried, 'What shall we do?
What's left won't even make a stew!'
And as she wept, her son was seen
To eat his head, his heart, his spleen.
And there he lay – a boy no more –
Just a stomach on the floor . . .
But none the less, since it *was* his,
They ate it – that's what haggis is.*

Terry Jones

---

* No it isn't. Haggis is a kind of stuffed pudding eaten by
the Scots. The minced heart, liver, lungs of a sheep, calf or
other animal's inner organs are mixed with oatmeal,
sealed and boiled in the maw (in the stomach-bag) of a
sheep and . . . excuse me a minute. *Ed.*

Diary of Wee Willie Winkie

Sunday
Couldn't sleep.
Got up and lit candle
ran upstairs, downstairs also
Ran round the town
Also, round the lady's chamber
Walked back home.
Still couldn't sleep.

Peter Dixon

29

Kids' Stuff

Hanging round parks for a go on the swings
your palms smelling of metal off the roundabout
The iron grip of the slide as you launch yourself
It's kids' stuff but I still like it.

Dipping your fingers in sherbet and licking
Sticking your tongue into your ice cream
Strengthening your suck on a McDonald's milk shake
It's kids' stuff but I still like it

Playing follow-my-leader when no one can see
Tidying your dollshouse and making them speak
Cuddling your teddy when you can't get to sleep
It's kids' stuff but I still like it

Reading Narnia books and travelling with Hobbits
Watching E. Nesbit's books on the box
Curling up in a chair with a book and some chocolate
It's kids' stuff but I still like it

Making shapes with your bread dough and watching it rise
Making gingerbread men with currants for eyes
Putting Smarties on top of little iced cakes
It's kids' stuff but I still like it

Going to the pictures to watch Walt Disney
Getting stick fingers from eating popcorn
Sucking an ice-lolly through the second half
It's kids' stuff but I still like it

People try and tell you you ought to grow up
My kids don't mind having a daft mum
I don't see why I should stop having fun
It's kids' stuff but I still like it.

Angela Topping

Nineteen Things to Do in Winter

Find the sledge in the back of the garage,
Grease the runners and paint it red.
Watch the weather report for news of snow.
Cuddle up in bed and read a book
that's as long as a long winter night.
Listen to the wind moan.
Keep an eye on the sky for snow clouds on the horizon.
Draw rude faces on steamed-up windows.
Go to football. Watch the Gunners. Groan and cheer.

Rescue fish in frozen ponds
And old ladies at the bottom of icy hills.
Drop an icicle down your sister's tights
Warm cold knees and icy bottom round roaring fire
Check the sky for snow.
Fit sledge with seats made from cushions of armchair in
    front room.
Make balls of fat and birdseed to feed the blue tits.
Be sympathetic when Dad fuses the lights.
Ring the meteorological office and ask when it's going to
    snow.
Paint go-faster stripes on sledge.
Say to Mum, I've no idea where the armchair cushions have
    gone.
Dream of green trees and buzzing bees and summer seas
Wonder why it hasn't snowed again this year.

Roger Stevens

December

This is Our House

This is our house
Called Violet Vista
And this is Susie, my horrible sister.
Dad's my father, and Mum's my mother
And this is Barry, my baby brother.
Grandad and Gran, Grandpa and Nan,
Aunt Eliza and Great-Aunt Nell
And all of my cousins live here as well –
There's Molly who's jolly
And Billie who's silly
And Jenny and Penny
And Georgie and Jilly
And Jessica June who eats cake with a spoon
And Gloria Rose with a spot on her nose
And Dolly who's tall
And Davie who's small
And Micky and Ricky the littlest of all.

Altogether that's twenty-three . . .
Just a moment.
Who have I forgotten?
Oh . . .
ME!

Vivian French

Embryonic Mega-Stars

We can play reggae music, funk and skiffle too,
We prefer heavy metal but the classics sometimes do.
We're keen on Tamla-Motown, folk and soul,
But most of all, what we like
Is basic rock and roll.
We can play the monochord, the heptachord and flute,
We're OK on the saxophone and think the glockenspiel is
    cute,
We really love the tuba, the balalaika and guitar
And our duets on the clavichord are bound to take us far.
We think castanets are smashing, harmonicas are fun,
And with the ocarina have only just begun.
We've mastered synthesizers, bassoons and violins
As well as hurdy-gurdies, pan-pipes and mandolins.
The tom-tom and the tabor, the trumpet and the drum
We learnt to play in between the tintinnabulum.
We want to form a pop group
And will when we're eleven,
But at the moment Tracey's eight
And I'm only seven.

Brian Patten

Bird-Table Blues

In Winter, Grandma feeds the birds
With kindly thoughts and friendly words,
And biscuit crumbs, and broken baps,
And bacon rinds, and breakfast scraps,
And plates of freshly buttered toast,
And bags of chips, and Sunday roast,
And dumplings (huge and hot and steamy),
And home-made pies, and gravy (creamy),
And every sort of cheese and bread,
Until each hungry bird is fed
To BURSTING point, to bitter end,
Until their legs begin to bend,
Until they cannot flap or fly,
Until they simply want to die,
Until they roll around the floor
And weakly twitter, 'Stop! No more!'

Then Grandma smiles and says, 'Oh good.
I think they're ready for their pud.'

Clare Bevan

4

Smile

Smile, go on, smile!
Anyone would think, to look at you,
that your cat was on the barbecue
or your best friend had died.
Go on, curve your mouth.
Take a look at that beggar,
or that one-legged bus conductor.
Where's *your* cross?
Smile, slap your thigh.
Hiccup, make a horse noise,
lollop through the house,
fizz up your coffee.
Take down your guitar
from its air-shelf and play
imaginary reggae
out through the open door.
And smile, remember, smile,
give those teeth some sun,
grin at everyone,
do it now, go on, SMILE!

Matthew Sweeney

Henry the Eighth

Henry the Eighth had six wives,
The reason was quite strange,
It wasn't that he loved them all,
He just loved to chop and change.

Valerie Bloom

Protection

I've got woollen underpants
And by Jove, I'm glad I've got 'em
'cos when you toboggan and slide in the snow
You can get a very cold bottom.

Roger Stevens

7

The Day We Built the Snowman

Round and round the garden
Rolling up the snow
One step, two step,
Watch the snowman grow.

Round and round the garden
Us and dad and mum,
Building up the snowman
Having lots of fun.

Mum has got a carrot,
Dad has got a pipe,
Sister's got a scarf
To keep him warm at night.

Baseball cap and shades,
Trainers for his feet,
Our trendy friendly snowman,
The coolest in the street.

Round and round the garden
In the Winter weather,
The day we built the snowman . . .
Having fun together.

Paul Cookson

8

Bauble Blues

o
o
o o
o o
oohhh!
it's not much
fun as a Christmas
decoration – I only work
one month a year and then
for the other eleven months
I'm stuffed into a box next
to old goody-two-shoes
the fairy – what a
life, eh?!

James Carter

9

Wanted

Wanted – a reliable star
to lead small party
westwards. Bright, with
good sense of direction.
Wage dependent on
experience. Send CV to
Wiseman, CHILDWATCH.

Sue Cowling

10

Curse of the Mistletoe

I stand beneath the mistletoe
and dream of kissing Mary
but all I get is Gran
and her nostrils that are hairy.

Paul Cookson

I'm Making a Hat for the Christmas Party

I'm
making
a hat for the
Christmas party
everyone makes a hat
but mine always seem to go lop-sided

Coral Rumble

A Plea from an Angel

'I want to be *different*!
I want to wear brown –
And strum on a banjo –
And fly upside down . . .'

Trevor Harvey

13

The Reverend Sabine Baring-Gould

The Reverend Sabine Baring-Gould,
  Rector (sometime) at Lew,
Once at a Christmas party asked,
  'Whose pretty child are you?'

(The Rector's family was long,
  His memory was poor,
And as to who was who had grown
  Increasingly unsure.)

At this, the infant on the stair
  Most sorrowfully sighed.
'Whose pretty little girl am I?
  Why, *yours*, papa!' she cried.

Charles Causley

The Reverend Sabine Baring-Gould (1834–1924) was
Rector for 43 years at Lewtrenchard in Devon. He is the
author of the hymn 'Onward, Christian soldiers'.

Merrily on High

Santa's trudging –
rooftop snow –
hidden chimney:
'Ho, Ho, H

o

o

o

o

o

!

Mike Johnson

The Christmas Spider

My fine web sparkles:
Indoor star in the roof's night
Over the baby.

Michael Richards

Just Doing My Job

I'm one of Herod's Henchmen.
We don't have much to say,
We just charge through the audience
In a Henchman sort of way.

We all wear woolly helmets
To hide our hair and ears,
And wellingtons sprayed silver
To match our tinfoil spears.

Our swords are made of cardboard
So blood will not be spilled
If we trip and stab a parent
When the hall's completely filled.

We don't look VERY scary,
We're mostly small and shy,
And some of us wear glasses,
But we give the thing a try.

We whisper Henchman noises
While Herod hunts for strangers,
And then we all charge out again
Like nervous Power Rangers.

Yet when the play is over
And Miss is out of breath
We'll charge like Henchmen through the hall
And scare our Mums to death.

Clare Bevan

17

The Wrong Words

We like to sing the wrong words
to Christmas Carols . . .

We three kings of Orient are,
One in a taxi, one in a car . . .

It drives our music teacher barmy,
his face turns red as a holly berry,
his forehead creases,
his eyes bulge.
It looks as if the top of his head
is about to lift like a saucepan lid
as he boils over . . .

His anger spills out
in an almighty shout . . .

'NO,' he roars . . .

'If you do that once more
I'll give you the kind of Christmas gift
you won't forget in a hurry . . .'

So we sing . . .
. . . *most highly flavoured lady* . . .

'IT'S FAVOURED,' he screams,
'NOT FLAVOURED . . .

What do you think she is,
an ice cream cone?'

Then to cap it all,
and drive him really wild
we sing of the shepherds
washing their socks,
till he slams down the piano lid
and takes off like a rocket
into the stratosphere,
lighting up the sky
like a Christmas star.

Brian Moses

We Three Kings

We three kings of Orient are,
One in a taxi,
One in a car,
One in a scooter,
Blowing his hooter,
Smoking a big cigar.

Anon.

Snow Storm

Oh, I am the King of the Snowmen,
I've lived here for years and for years.
I've never been slushy,
Or melted, or mushy,
Or changed to a puddle of tears.

Oh, I am the King of the Snowmen,
I'm jolly and shiny and fat.
My home, small yet classy,
Has skies blue and glassy,
And snowstorms that swirl round my hat.

Oh, I am the King of the Snowmen,
I've never been known to complain,
But sometimes my world shakes
With TERRIBLE earthquakes . . .
Take cover! They've started again!

Clare Bevan

Dear Father Christmas

Dear Father Christmas
This year please bring me
A pet rhinoc . . .
rhisoser . . .
rhinisus
rhinsiocerus
rhisky hoperus
rhibsipoperus
er . . .
I've changed my mind.
Bring me a rabbit instead.

Roger Stevens

21

Who Drops Down the Chimney?

Cats get visits from Santa Paws
Sharks listen out for Santa Jaws
Crabs hope for gifts from Santa Claws
Crows' stockings are filled by Santa Caws

Footballers cheer for Santa Scores
Sailors sigh for Santa Shores
Judges wait for Santa Laws
Carpenters wish for Santa Saws

But up in my bedroom, behind closed doors
I'm busy dreaming of Santa Snores.

John Coldwell

22

Reindeer Report

Chimneys: colder.
Flightpaths: busier.
Driver: Christmas (F)
Still baffled by postcodes.

Children: more
And stay up later.
Presents: heavier.
Pay: frozen.

Mission in spite
Of all this
Accomplished:
Merry Christmas!

U. A. Fanthorpe

We Are Not Alone

Captain's Log. Starship Saturnalian.
Earth year 2030, day 358 –
The new drive worked! We've tracked the alien
spacecraft that vanished from Earth's orbit late

last night. We followed its fantastic leap
across the galaxy and now can see
its sledge-like shape dropping in steep
descent to a planet. Incredibly

a single cosmonaut whose suit glows red
clings to its tail and holds long ropes to steer
a group of prancing creatures: from each head
sprout aerials that make them look like deer.

The planet's steaming, its surfaces smooth and
dark as Christmas pudding. Prepare to land!

Dave Calder

24

fr xmas' txt msg

where r u? mrsx
lost. frx
where lost? mrsx
fi nu I wunt be lost. fr x
nt funny. diner n'ly redi. mrsx
rudolph nose went out in fog. lost. frx
told u it ws goin dim!!! still fogi? mrsx
no – fog gone bt dunt recognise were am now. frx
describe. mrsx
big pointy stone things and camels. frx
u in Egypt. mrsx
2morrow I sack rudolph. frx
i give dinner to elves. mrsx
i is sorry. frx
nt haf as sorry as u will be!!! mrsx

Mike Harding

Christmas Pudding

It lay on the table
proudly displayed.
'The best Christmas pudding,'
said Mum, 'ever made.

'You'll all find out
just how good in a minute,
for I've put some special
ingredients in it.'

It did seem sort
of strange somehow.
I couldn't quite
describe it now –

like something from
the fourth dimension.
'It is,' said Mum,
'my own invention.

'You'll all remember
this – don't doubt it!'
Gran peered. 'There's something
odd about it.'

'Well, here we go,'
smiled Mum with pride
and grasped the knife
that lay beside.

'This is how puddings
should be made.'
The candlelight
gleamed off the blade.

There was a hush.
Time seemed to stop.
The knife blade touched
the pudding top.

The room shook in
a blinding flash,
a huge bang
and a mighty crash.

'Aliens!' I thought.
'Is my laser loaded?'
But no – the pudding
had exploded.

We sat there stunned
in frozen poses.
Bits of it
were up our noses.

Mum looked very
close to tears.
Bits of it
were in our ears.

Bits of it
dropped down the chair.
Bits of it
were in our hair.

Still no one moved
from where we sat.
Bits of it
were on the cat.

'Well then,' said Dad,
'no need to wait.'
Yes – bits of it
were on each plate.

'You're right, dear. Each
year in December,
this is a dish
that we'll remember.'

Bits covered the table
like lumpy lacquer.
'Very clever – a Christmas
pudding cracker.'

Charles Thomson

Christmas Cinquain Thank You

Thanks Gran
Loved the pink rose
Scented bubble bath and
Perfume, shame you forgot I'm your
Grandson

Paul Cookson

Jabberwocky

'Twas brillig, and the slithy toves
    Did gyre and gimble in the wabe;
All mimsy were the borogoves,
    And the mome raths outgrabe.

'Beware the Jabberwock, my son!
    The jaws that bite, the claws that catch!
Beware the Jubjub bird, and shun
    The frumious Bandersnatch!'

He took his vorpal sword in hand:
    Long time the manxome foe he sought –
So rested he by the Tumtum tree,
    And stood awhile in thought.

And as in uffish thought he stood,
    The Jabberwock, with eyes of flame,
Came whiffling through the tulgey wood,
    And burbled as it came!

One, two! One, two! And through and through
    The vorpal blade went snicker-snack!
He left it dead, and with its head
    He went galumphing back.

'And hast thou slain the Jabberwock?
　　Come to my arms, my beamish boy!
O frabjous day! Callooh! Callay!'
　　He chortled in his joy.

'Twas brillig, and the slithy toves
　　Did gyre and gimble in the wabe;
All mimsy were the borogoves,
　　And the mome raths outgrabe.

Lewis Carroll

The Day After The Day After
Boxing Day

On the day after the day after Boxing Day
Santa wakes up, eventually,
puts away his big red suit and wellies,
lets Rudolph and the gang out into the meadow
then shaves his head and beard.

December

He puts on his new cool sunglasses,
baggy blue Bermuda shorts (he's sick of red),
yellow stripy T-shirt that doesn't quite cover his belly
and lets his toes breathe in flip-flops.

Packing a bucket and spade,
fifteen tubes of Factor Twenty suncream
and seventeen romantic novels
he fills his Walkman with the latest sounds,
is glad to use a proper suitcase instead of the old sack
and heads off into the Mediterranean sunrise
enjoying the comforts of a Boeing 747
(although he passes on the free drinks).

Six months later,
relaxed, red and a little more than stubbly,
he looks at his watch, adjusts his wide-brimmed sunhat,
mops the sweat from his brow and strokes his chin,
wondering why holidays always seem to go so quickly.

Paul Cookson

29

The Snowman

Once there was a snowman
Stood outside the door
Thought he'd like to come inside
And run around the floor;
Thought he'd like to warm himself
By the firelight red;
Thought he'd like to climb up
On that big white bed.
So he called the North Wind, 'Help me now, I pray.
I'm completely frozen, standing here all day.'
So the North Wind came along and blew him in the door,
And now there's nothing left of him
But a puddle on the floor!

Anon.

Who Said What
(Conversation Poem)

To the boy with his head
Stuck through the railings in the park,

The Optimist said:	Don't worry, son, we'll soon have you out.
The Psychiatrist said:	How do you feel?
The Photographer said:	Smile please!
The Counsellor said:	Would you care to talk about it?
The Pessimist said:	You might never get out.
The Blacksmith said:	Nice piece of ironwork.
The Traffic Warden said:	You can't stay there.
The Sympathizer said:	I know just how you feel.
The Stoic said:	Just grin and bear it.
The Clairvoyant said:	I thought this might happen.
The Newspaper Reporter said:	HEADLINE – BOY IN PARK RAILING ORDEAL!
The Philosopher said:	It's merely a state of mind.
The Job's Comforter said:	You've probably damaged your neck.
The Joker said:	Don't go away.
The Realist said:	You've got your head stuck.

But the boy with his head
Stuck through the railings in the park said simply:
GET ME OUT!

Gervase Phinn

Hush Hush

Norman is
a
secret agent.
Only family
and
close friends
know this.
Those of you
who have read
this poem
please
destroy it
and
forget
you ever
saw
it.

John C. Desmond

Index of First Lines

431

Index of First Lines

Index of First Lines

Index of Poets

Index of Poets

Acknowledgements

The compiler and publisher wish to thank the following for permission to use copyright material:

Allan Ahlberg, 'Please Mrs Butler' from *Please Mrs Butler* by Allan Ahlberg, Kestrel (1983). Copyright © Allan Ahlberg, 1983, by permission of Penguin Books Ltd; **Philip Ardagh**, 'Batty About Bats' and 'Antelopes', by permission of the author; **David Bateman**, 'School for Spring', first published in *Spectacular Schools*, eds. Paul Cookson and David Harmer, Macmillan (2004). Copyright © David Bateman, 2002, by permission of the author; **Hilaire Belloc**, 'Matilda' from *Cautionary Verse* by Hilaire Belloc, Red Fox, by permission of PFD on behalf of the estate of the author; **Gerard Benson**, 'Fishing' and 'A Tale of Two Citizens' from *To Catch an Elephant* by Gerard Benson, Smith-Doorstop (2002), 'My Spaniel' and 'Second Look at the Proverbs', by permission of the author; **John Betjeman**, 'Hunter Trials' from *Collected Poems* by John Betjeman, by permission of John Murray Ltd; **Clare Bevan**, 'Literacy Hour' and 'April 1st' from *Teacher's Revenge*, ed. Brian Moses, Macmillan (2003), 'Letters to the Three Pigs' from *Are You Sitting Comfortably?*, ed. Brian Moses, Macmillan (2002), 'Just Doing My Job' from *We Three Kings*, ed. Brian Moses, Macmillan (1998), 'When the Aliens Came to Dinner', to be published in *Space Poems*, ed. John Foster, Macmillan, 'Monster Sale', to be published in *Monster Poems*, Macmillan, 'Bird Table Blues' and 'Snowstorm', by permission of the author; **Valerie Bloom**, 'Chicken Poxed', 'Haircut Rap' and 'Henry the Eighth' from *Let Me Touch the Sky* by Valerie Bloom, Macmillan (2000) by permission of Eddison Pearson Ltd on behalf of the author; **Tony Bradman**, 'Starter' and 'Two Lists' from *Smile, Please* by Tony Bradman, Viking Kestrel (1987). Copyright © Tony Bradman, 1987, 'The Sweet' from *All Together Now* by Tony Bradman, Penguin Books. Copyright © Tony Bradman, 1989, by permission of The Agency (London) Ltd on behalf of the author; **Paul Bright**, 'Up in Smoke', first published in *Shorts*, ed. Paul Cookson, Macmillan Children's Books (2000), 'A Small Dragon Verse', first published in *Ha Ha! 100 Poems to Make You Laugh*, ed. Paul Cookson, Macmillan (2003), by permission of the author; **Liz Brownlee**, 'Purrfect', 'Hippobotamus', 'Shoem', 'The Ghoul Inspectre's Coming' and 'Puffer Fish', by permission of the author; **Dave Calder**, 'We Are Not Alone', by permission of the author; **Richard Caley**, 'Blow-Dry Bill's a Baddie', by permission of the author; **James Carter**, 'Garden Shed' and 'Bauble Blues' from *Cars, Stars and Electric Guitars* by James Carter. Copyright © 2002 James Carter, by permission of Walker Books Ltd; 'Sorry, Sorry, Sorry' and 'Icy Morning Haikus', by permission of the author; **Charles Causley**, 'There Once Was a Man', 'I Saw a Jolly Hunter', 'Colonel Fazackerley' and

447

Acknowledgements

'The Reverend Sabine Baring-Gould' from *Collected Poems for Children* by Charles Causley, Macmillan, by permission of David Higham Associates on behalf of the author; **Debjani Chatterjee**, 'Postcard from Lilliput', first published in *Mice on Ice: A World Book Day Poetry Book*, ed. Gaby Morgan, Macmillan (2004), by permission of the author; **Alison Chisholm**, 'Love Letter', by permission of the author; **John Coldwell**, 'Two Witches Discuss Good Grooming', first published in *Read Me* 2, ed. Gaby Morgan, Macmillan (1999), and 'A Visit to Yalding' from *Are You Sitting Comfortably?*, ed. Brian Moses, Macmillan (2002), 'My Chat Up Technique Needs Attention', 'Where's That Gorilla?' and 'Who Drops Down The Chimney', by permission of the author; **Bill Condon**, 'Aunt Brute' from *Don't Throw Rocks at Chickenpox* by Bill Condon, Angus and Robertson (1993), by permission of the author; **Paul Cookson**, 'Short Visit, Long Stay' and 'My Uncle Percy Once Removed' from *The Very Best of Paul Cookson*, Macmillan (2001), 'It Wasn't Me', 'I've Seen Mrs Newton's Knickers', 'Arthur, My Half-Cousin', 'Epitaph for the Last Martian', 'A Sumo Wrestler Chappy', 'I Would Win the Gold . . .', 'The Day After The Day After Boxing Day', 'Bus Queue', 'There Was an Art Teacher from Bude', 'The Day We Built the Snowman', 'Curse of the Mistletoe' and 'Christmas Cinquain', by permission of the author; **Sue Cowling**, 'Ghoul School Rules', 'Words Behaving Badly' and 'Wanted', by permission of the author; **Roald Dahl**, 'Little Red Riding Hood and the Wolf' from *Revolting Rhymes* by Roald Dahl, Jonathan Cape and Penguin Books, by permission of David Higham Associates on behalf of the estate of the author; **Ian Deal**, 'Somewhere', by permission of the author; **Jan Dean**, 'Gift' and 'Grandma' from *Wallpapering the Cat* by Jan Dean, Macmillan (2003), 'Hello Mrs Morley', 'Aaaaargh', by permission of the author; **Graham Denton**, 'A Bit of a Low Point', 'All The Trappings' and 'A Butter Bother', by permission of the author; **John C. Desmond**, 'Hush Hush' from *My Stepdad Is an Alien*, ed. David Harmer, Macmillan (2003), 'We All Have to Go' and 'Cry for Help', by permission of the author; **Peter Dixon**, 'Before the Days of Noah', 'Magic Cat', 'For Brownie (the goldfish)', 'Where Do All the Teachers Go?', 'Lost Voice', 'Fear', 'House Party', 'Diary of Jack', 'Diary of Jill', 'Diary of Cock Robin', and 'Diary of Wee Willie Winkie', by permission of the author; **Lord Alfred Douglas**, 'The Shark' and 'The Cod', by permission of John Rubinstein and John Stratford, Joint Literary Executors of the estate of the author; **Gina Douthwaite**, 'Shoe Boot! Shoe' and 'Knickers' from *Picture a Poem* by Gina Douthwaite, Red Fox (1996), by permission of Random House Group Ltd and Andrew Mann Ltd on behalf of the author; **Richard Edwards**, 'Oh, Ozzie!' from *The House That Caught a Cold* by Richard Edwards, Viking (1991), 'The Blue Room', by permission of the author; **U. A. Fanthorpe**, 'Reindeer Report' from *Christmas Poems* by U. A. Fanthorpe (2002), by permission of Peterloo Poets; **Max Fatchen**, 'Look Out!'. Copyright © Max Fatchen, by permission of Johnson & Alcock Ltd on behalf of the author; **Eric Finney**, 'Didn't He Dance', by permission of the author; **Michael Flanders**, 'The Hippopotamus Song'. Copyright © 1952 Chappell Music Ltd, London, by permission of International Music Publications Ltd; **John Foster**, 'Borrowed Time' and 'My Baby Brother's Secrets' from *Climb Aboard the Poetry Plane* by John Foster, Oxford University Press. Copyright © 2000 John Foster, 'Sandra Slater' from *Word Wizard* by John Foster, Oxford University Press. Copyright © 2001 John Foster, 'Dad's Hiding in the Shed' from *Making Waves* by John Foster, Oxford University Press. Copyright © 2001 John Foster, by permission of the author; **Vivian French**, 'This Is Our House', by permission of Fraser Ross Associates on behalf of the author; **Andrew Fusek Peters**, 'In Training', first published in *On a Camel to the Moon*, ed. Valerie Bloom, Belitha Press (2003), 'Junk Uncle' and 'E-PET-APH' from *Sadderday and Funday* by Andrew Fusek Peters and Polly Peters, Hodder (2001), by permission of the author; **Chrissie Gittins**, 'Government Health Warning', by permission of the author; **Mick Gowar**, 'The Magician's Garden', 'The Clown's Garden' and 'The Flight of the Bumble Bee', by permission of the author; **Gus Grenfell**, 'My Mates', by permission of the author; **Mike Harding**, 'fr xmas' txt msg', by permission of the author; **David Harmer**, 'Mr Moore', 'Help!', 'The Lone Teacher', 'Seven Solemn and Serious Superstitions', 'The Ferret Poem', 'Playing Tennis With Justin', 'The PM is 10 Today' and 'Mum's Put Me on the Transfer List', by permission of the author; **Michael Harrison**, 'Miss! Sue Is Kissing', by permission of J. M. Gibson; **Anne Harvey**, 'Twin Trouble' from *The Naughtiest Children I Know*, ed. Anne Harvey, Red Fox (2000), by permission of the author; **Trevor Harvey**, 'The Painting Lesson', first published in *Children's Poems*, ed. Heather Amery, Usborne (1990), 'A Plea from an Angel', first published in *The Rhyme Riot*, ed. Gaby Morgan, Macmillan (2002), 'Cliches', first published in *Don't Get Your Knickers in a Twist*, ed. Paul Cookson, Macmillan (2002), and 'Here's What They Are', by permission of the author; **Adrian Henri**, 'A Poem for My Cat' from *The Phantom Lollipop Lady* by Adrian Henri, Methuen Books (1986). Copyright © Adrian Henri 1986, by permission of Rogers, Coleridge & White Ltd on behalf of the author; **Ted Hughes**, 'Stickleback' from *Collected Animal Poems: Volume 1 The Iron Wolf* by Ted Hughes, by permission of Faber and Faber Ltd; **Mike Johnson**, 'Practical Science', 'Invisible Boy', 'Dad, the Amateur Hypnotist', 'Science Lesson' and 'Merrily on High', by permission of the author; **Terry Jones**, 'Horace', by permission of the author; **Mike Jubb**, 'Not Funny', by permission of the author; **Stephen Knight**, 'Last' from *Dream City Cinema* by Stephen Knight (1996), by permission of Bloodaxe Books; and 'Sardines' from *Sardines and Other Poems* by Stephen Knight (2004), by permission of Macmillan; **Tony Langham**, 'Although', first published in *Don't Get Your Knickers in a Twist*, ed. Paul Cookson (2002*)*, by permission of the author; **Patricia Leighton**, 'Letter to a Dead Dog', by permission of the author; **Roger McGough**, 'Mafia Cats' from *Bad Bad Cats*, Viking. Copyright © Roger McGough 1987, 'Wiwis' from *An Imaginary*

Acknowledgements

Menagerie by Roger McGough, Viking. Copyright © Roger McGough, 1988, 'Sky in the Pie!', 'The Leader', 'Fire Guard' and 'The Cabbage Is a Funny Veg' from *Sky in the Pie* by Roger McGough, Kestrel. Copyright © Roger McGough 1983, 'No Peas for the Wicked' from *Lucky* by Roger McGough, Viking. Copyright © Roger McGough 1993, and 'A Good Poem' from *In the Glassroom* by Roger McGough. Copyright © Roger McGough 1976; by permission of PFD on behalf of the author; **Ian McMillan**, 'Counting the Stars', 'An Interesting Fact about One of my Relatives', 'No Bread', 'Some Sayings That Never Caught on', 'Robinson Crusoe's Wise Sayings' and 'Batman's Exercise Video', by permission of the author; **Lindsay MacRae**, 'Do We Have to Kiss', 'Worst Sellers' and 'The Giggles' from *How to Make a Snail Fall In Love With You* by Lindsay MacRae, Puffin Books (2003) and 'The Babysitter', 'The Thingy' and 'When I Was Young' from *How to Avoid Kissing Your Parents in Public* by Lindsay MacRae, Puffin Books (2000), by permission of the author; **George Macbeth**, 'The Red Herring', by permission of Sheil Land Associates Ltd on behalf of the estate of the author; **Wes Magee**, 'Cemetery Epitaph', by permission of the author; **Gerda Mayer**, 'Ice-Cream Poem', first published in *New Statesman Weekend Comp.*, 9.8.58, by permission of the author; **Spike Milligan**, 'Bump', 'Baby Sardine', 'On the Ning Nang Nong', 'Today I Saw a Little Worm' and 'Granny', by permission of Spike Milligan Productions Ltd; **Trevor Millum**, 'Jabbermockery', 'Sunday in the Yarm Fard', 'Dick's Dog', 'Match of the Year' and 'The Dark Avenger', by permission of the author; **Adrian Mitchell**, 'Fruit Jokes' from *All My Own Stuff* by Adrian Mitchell, Hodder Wayland. Copyright © Adrian Mitchell 1991, by permission of PFD on behalf of the author; **Tony Mitton**, 'Make a Face', by permission of David Higham Associates on behalf of the author; **John Mole**, 'The Uncomfortable Truth' from *The Conjuror's Rabbit*, ed. John Mole, Blackie (1992), 'First Love' from *Hot Air*, ed. John Mole, Hodder (1996), 'Gnomic' and 'The Pong' from *The Dummy's Dilemma*, ed. John Mole, Hodder (1999), and 'Answer Phone' from *The Wonder Dish*, ed. John Mole, Oxford University Press (2002), by permission of the author; **Brian Moses**, 'What Teachers Wear in Bed', 'Aliens Stole My Underpants' and 'The Wrong Words', by permission of the author; **Ogden Nash**, 'The Parent', 'The Adventures of Isabel', 'Next', 'The Germ', 'The Fly', 'The Cow', 'The Dog' and 'The Duck' from *Candy Is Dandy: The Best of Ogden Nash* by Ogden Nash, intro. Anthony Burgess. Copyright ©, first publication, 1933, 1936, 1953, 1933, 1942, 1931, 1957, 1954 by Ogden Nash, renewed, by permission of Andre Deutsch Ltd and Curtis Brown, Ltd on behalf of the author; and 'The Mermaid'. Copyright © 1941 by Ogden Nash, renewed, by permission of Curtis Brown, Ltd on behalf of the estate of the author; **Grace Nichols**, 'My Cousin Melda' from *Come on into My Tropical Garden* by Grace Nichols. Copyright © 1988 by Grace Nichols, by permission of Curtis Brown, Ltd on behalf of the author; **Alfred Noyes**, 'Daddy Fell into the Pond', by permission of The Society of Authors as the

450

Acknowledgements

Literary Representative of the estate of the author; **David Orme**, 'Hogging Hedgehogs' and 'Larks with Sharks', by permission of the author; **Gareth Owen**, 'Basil', 'Crocodile', 'Come on in the Water's Lovely', 'Miss Creedle Teaches Creative Writing', 'Wellingtons' and 'Scatterbrain' from *Collected Poems for Children* by Gareth Owen, Macmillan (2000). Copyright © Gareth Owen 2000, by permission of Rogers, Coleridge & White on behalf of the author; **Brian Patten**, 'Embyonic Mega-Stars' from *Gargling with Jelly* by Brian Patten, Viking (1985). Copyright © Brian Patten 1985, by permission The Penguin Group (UK) Ltd and Rogers, Coleridge & White Ltd on behalf of the author, 'The Day I Got My Finger Stuck up My Nose' from *Juggling with Gerbils* by Brian Patten, Puffin Books (2000). Copyright © Brian Patten 2000, 'The Rival Arrives' and 'The Invisible Man's Invisible Dog' from *Thawing Frozen Frogs* by Brian Patten, Puffin Books (1992). Copyright © Brian Patten 1992, by permission of Rogers, Coleridge & White on behalf of the author; **Noel Petty**, 'What For', first published in *This Poem Doesn't Rhyme*, ed. Gerard Benson, Puffin Books. Copyright © Noel Petty 1990, by permission of Campbell, Thomson & McLaughlin Ltd on behalf of the author; **Gervase Phinn**, 'Today I Feel', 'Who Said What' and 'Interrogation', by permission of the author; **Jack Prelutsky**, 'A Piglet' and 'I Built a Fabulous Machine' from *It's Raining Pigs and Noodles* by Jack Prelutsky. Copyright © 2000 by Jack Prelutsky, by permission of HarperCollins Publishers; **Julia Rawlinson**, 'Timetable', by permission of the author; **James Reeves**, 'Doctor Emmanuel' from *Complete Poems for Children* by James Reeves. Copyright © James Reeves 1950, by permission of Laura Cecil Literary Agency on behalf of the estate of the author; **John Rice**, 'Ettykett', 'Instructions for Giants', 'The Mysteries of Nature', 'History Lesson: Part 2 – The Romans' and 'The Hungry Wolf', by permission of the author; **Laura E. Richards**, 'Eletelephony' from *Tirra Lirra* by Laura Richards. Copyright © 1930, 1932 Laura Richards. Copyright © renewed 1960 by Hamilton Richards, by permission of Little, Brown and Company, Inc; **Cynthia Rider**, 'Heather Potts', by permission of the author; **Rachel Rooney**, 'Property for Sale', by permission of the author; **Michael Rosen**, 'Running' from *You Wait Till I'm Older Than You!* by Michael Rosen, Viking. Copyright © Michael Rosen 1996, 'Me and My Brother' and 'Hot Food' from *The Hypnotiser* by Michael Rosen, Andre Deutsch Ltd. Copyright © Michael Rosen 1988, 'I'm carrying the Baby' from *Don't Put Mustard in the Custard* by Michael Rosen. Copyright © 1985, and 'Thirty Days Hath September' from *Hairy Tales and Nursery Crimes* by Michael Rosen, Andre Deutsch Ltd. Copyright © 1985, by permission of PFD on behalf of the author; **Coral Rumble**, 'Revenge' and 'I'm Making a Hat for the Christmas Party', by permission of the author; **Fred Sedgwick**, 'Auntie's Boyfriend' and 'Victoria's Poem' from *Blind Date* by Fred Sedgwick, Tricky Sam! Press, 'What the Headteacher Said' from *Two by Two* by John Cotton and Fred Sedgwick, Mary Glasgow Publications, 'Notice on a

Acknowledgements

Classroom Door', 'Nine Reasons for Hating Children' and 'Fall in Love', by permission of the author; **Andy Seed**, 'Hindsight', first published in *Funny Poems*, ed. Jan Dean, Scholastic (2003), by permission of the author; **Andrea Shavick**, 'Auntie Betty Thinks She's Batgirl', 'Batgirl's Disgrace', 'How to successfully persuade . . .' and 'Grandma Was Eaten by a Shark', by permission of the author; **Shel Silverstein**, 'It's Dark in Here' from *Where the Sidewalk Ends* by Shel Silverstein. Copyright © 1974 by Evil Eye Music, Inc, by permission of Edite Kroll Literary Agency, Inc on behalf of the estate of the author; **Lemn Sissay**, 'When I'm Older', by permission of the author; **Roger Stevens**, 'A Dog's Day' from *Don't Get Your Knickers in a Twist*, ed. Paul Cookson, Macmillan (2002), 'My Stepdad Is an Alien' and 'Flares' from *My Stepdad Is an Alien*, ed. David Harmer, Macmillan (2002), 'Taking My Human for a Walk' from *Taking My Human for a Walk*, ed. Roger Stevens, Macmillan (2003), 'Introducing Dad', 'A Sticky Riddle', 'Dragon Love Poem', 'Superheroes I Could Have Been', 'Cat Message', 'Escape Plane', 'Nineteen Things to Do in Winter', 'Protection' and 'Dear Father Christmas', by permission of the author; **Matthew Sweeney**, 'Smile' from *Up on the Roof* by Matthew Sweeney (2001), by permission of Faber and Faber Ltd, and 'Poem Spoken by a Cat', by permission of the author; **Marian Swinger**, 'Why' from *My Stepdad Is an Alien*, ed. David Harmer, Macmillan (2002), 'The Pupil Control Gadget' from *The Teacher's Revenge*, ed. Brian Moses, Macmillan (2003), 'Fairytale Princess School' and 'Mrs Goodwin's Part-time Job', by permission of the author; **Charles Thomson**, 'Christmas Pudding', by permission of the author; **Nick Toczek**, 'The Dragon Who Ate Our School', 'Seasick' and 'The Dragon in the Cellar', by permission of the author; **Angela Topping**, 'Finding Magic' and 'Winter Morning', by permission of the author; **Jill Townsend**, 'My Man Jeffrey', first published in *Taking My Human for a Walk*, ed. Roger Stevens, Macmillan (2003), by permission of the author; **Steve Turner**, 'New Year's Resolution' from *Dad, You're Not Funny* by Steve Turner (1999). Copyright © 1999 Steve Turner, and 'Assembly' from *Poems* by Steve Turner (2002). Copyright © 2002 Steve Turner, by permission of Lion Hudson plc; **Kaye Umansky**, 'My Father Is a Werewolf' from *Witches in Stiches* by Kaye Umansky, Puffin (1988), by permission of Caroline Sheldon Literary Agency on behalf of the author; **Philip Waddell**, 'Burying the Hatchet' from *Don't Get Your Knickers in a Twist*, ed. Paul Cookson, Macmillan (2002), 'Dad's a Superhero' from *My Stepdad Is an Alien*, ed. David Harmer, Macmillan (2002), and 'St Valentine's Day Massacre', by permission of the author; **Dave Ward**, 'It Makes Dad Mad', by permission of the author; **Celia Warren**, 'Neversaurus', 'Where's Grandma?', 'Ark Angels' and 'Elephantasy', by permission of the author; **Clive Webster**, 'The Greatest of Them All' from *My Stepdad Is an Alien*, ed. David Harmer, Macmillan (2002), by permission of the author; **Colin West**, 'She Likes to Swim Beneath the Sea', 'Elizabeth I', 'Coathanger', 'My Sister Sybil', 'King Arthur's Knights', 'Kate' and 'The Blunderbat', by

Acknowledgements

permission of the author; **Kit Wright**, 'Song Sung by a Man on a Barge' from *Hot Dog and Other Poems* by Kit Wright, Kestrel (1981). Copyright © Kit Wright, 1981, by permission of Penguin Books Ltd.

Every effort has been made to trace the copyright holders but if any have been inadvertently overlooked the publishers will be pleased to make the necessary arrangement at the first opportunity.